Seeing Through the World

A Nuralogical book,
produced in collaboration with Nura Learning
www.nuralearning.com

SEEING THROUGH THE WORLD:
Jean Gebser
and
Integral
Consciousness

Jeremy Johnson

REVELORE
MMXIX

Seeing Through the World:
Jean Gebser and Integral Consciousness

© Jeremy Johnson 2019

Book and cover design by Jenn Zahrt.
Cover image by Nina Bunjavec.

ISBN 978-1-947544-15-4
Printed globally on demand through IngramSpark

First printed by REVELORE PRESS in 2019

REVELORE PRESS
220 2ND AVE S #91
Seattle, WA 98104
USA

www.revelore.press

"Our concern is with a new reality—a reality functioning and effectual integrally, in which intensity and action, the effective and the effect co-exist; one where origin, by virtue of 'presentation,' blossoms forth anew; and one in which the present is all-encompassing and entire. Integral reality is the world's transparency, a perceiving of the world as truth: a mutual perceiving and imparting of truth of the world and of the human and of all that transluces both."
— Jean Gebser, *Ever-Present Origin*, 7.

"The book is addressed to each and every one, particularly those who live knowledge, and not just to those who create it."
—Gebser, *EPO*, xxviii.

To:

*My mother, father, and brother
for teaching me about origins and setting me on my path.*

*My wife, Natalie, for her loving support
and daily encouragement.*

*The International Jean Gebser Society:
they've taught me everything I know.*

·

*The integral world, that ever-present reality,
which informs this work and to which
all my efforts are dedicated.*

Acknowledgments

I would like to thank Jenn Zahrt, my friend and editor, who encouraged and then worked with me to create this book. It is an honor to further the availability of secondary literature on Jean Gebser in the English speaking world—Gebser's time is truly present, and prescient, and I hope that more follows.

The International Jean Gebser Society deserves my greatest thanks. My fellow "Gebserians" have served as collective mentors for me since I began attending the annual conferences in October of 2013. Much of what I have presented in this book is due in no small part to the enlightening and inspiriting conversations we have shared each year, hopping from conference venues—from Los Angeles, to Seattle, and New York—turning over the endless exegesis of meaning in *The Ever-Present Origin*, and exploring the nature of integral consciousness in our challenging time.

The spiritual and philosophical work of Jean Gebser, Pierre Teilhard de Chardin, Sri Aurobindo and Mirra Alfassa have been foundational for me as a thinker and even spiritual for me as a personal, evolutionary cosmology.

Great thanks goes to William Irwin Thompson, whose work and writing has been foundational for me and whom I am grateful to continue to exchange ideas and insights with.

Deep appreciation also goes to John David Ebert, John Dotson, Michael Purdy, Dave Zuckerman, Hans Gruenig, Sabrina Dalla Valle, J.F. Martel, Matthew T. Segall, Marco Morelli, Lisa Maroski, Gary Lachman, Heather Fester, Peter Weston, Brandt Stickley, Donna Schill, and Glenn Aparicio

Parry for our continued conversations and/or suggestions in helping this book along its way.

The 2018 Integral European Conference in Hungary—in which I was honored to present a talk at—was another major boon for interest in Gebser. Many attendees there had expressed enthusiastic interest in reading more about the structures of consciousness and sought a "Gebser 101" style introduction, and so this book owes much to their enthusiasm. I am grateful for the many years of dialogue with the Integral Theory community in the United States and abroad, and to the writings of Ken Wilber where, long ago, I discovered a literary portal to Gebser, Teilhard, Aurobindo, et al.

Finally, I would like to thank *all* my Patreon patrons for ongoing engagement and support, with special thanks to those at the "Super Team" tier and up: Alice Gormley, Alise Vanhecke, Conner Habib, David W. Pryor, Fred van Heukelom, Jeff Salzman, Nathan Snyder, Peter Weston, Riina Raudne, Samantha Leskie, and Tim Mansfield.

Contents

1

Towards an Integral Philosophy of the Present

> *Time is being and being*
> *time, it is all one thing,*
> *the shining, the seeing,*
> *the dark abounding.*
> — Ursula K. Le Guin[1]

JEAN GEBSER (1905–1973) was a German-Swiss cultural philosopher, intellectual mystic, poet, and scholar of the evolution of consciousness. Many know him in the English-speaking world for his magisterial text *The Ever-Present Origin* (1949–1952), a massive tome spanning art, language, and human history with great detail. Though perhaps lesser known than C. G. Jung, Erich Von Neumann (*Origins and History of Consciousness*), Pierre Teilhard de Chardin (*The Human*

---

1 Ursula K. Le Guin, *Late in the Day: Poems 2010–2014* (Oakland: PM Press, 2016), Kindle edition, 251.

Phenomenon), or Sri Aurobindo Ghose (*The Life Divine*), Gebser nevertheless offers immense insights for scholars and students of the evolution of consciousness alike. Spanning through the mid-twentieth century, Gebser saw his time, which is arguably *also* ours, as one of tremendous potentiation catalyzed by crisis. A solution *within* dissolution, and a *latent* spiritual mutation in humanity working towards realization. This incipient integral age—the "integral aperspectival" as a term I will attempt to introduce and convey to the reader in this volume—is nothing short of a leap from civilization as we know it (to *what*, we know not yet). It is an age unfathomable to us, however necessary, one in which Gebser suggests to us that, "the divided human being is replaced by the whole human being."[2] Key to understanding this leap is not mere intellectual comprehension alone but a form of spiritual *clarity*, a recognition of wholeness, a *waring* of past, present, and future. At the outset, the integral is an *intensification* of originary presence in the human person.

In the rolling thunder of the immanent present, all that we *are*, all that we *have been*, and all that we *could be* is radically *with* us.

---

2   Georg Feuerstein, *Structures of Consciousness* (Lower Lake: Integral Publishing, 1987), 170. Translation.

Time is whole and therefore *you* are whole.

Although coming to him in a "lightning-like" flash of inspiration in the early 1930s, Gebser's integral insight would need to be carefully articulated through many years of maturation and personal growth.[3] What began as a description of the *current* mutation, following the breakdown of Europe with the eruption of fascism and two World Wars and the simultaneous promise of a new form of consciousness expressed in the poetry of Rainer Maria Rilke or the post-Newtonian science of quantum physics, it expanded to include a study of *other* epochal shifts in human history. For instance: the leap from the *mythical* to the *mental* structure through the example of Socrates in Ancient Greece (Marshall McLuhan, the media theorist famous for "the medium is the message," has been compared with Gebser, and would draw similar conclusions about a leap in "sense ratios" through the advent of the Greek alphabetic script and systems of writing).[4] Gebser would come to describe these qualitatively different world spaces that are no less *real* than our own, with *phenomenologically* unique relationships to time and

---

3   Ibid., 25.

4   William Irwin Thompson, *Coming into Being: Artifacts and Texts in the Evolution of Consciousness* (New York: St. Martin's Press: 1996), 14.

space, as the *structures of consciousness*. These, briefly, are the archaic, magic, mythic, mental, and integral— each one a fundamental reworking of what it means to be in the world, and what the world *is* for us ontologically (meaning, in philosophy, a study of the nature of *being*). The structures, for the sensitive reader, are not merely categorical (i.e., the structuralism of Claude Lévi-Strauss and the social sciences[5]), they are living *realities* immediately apprehensible within oneself. Indeed, one of the prerequisites for Gebser's integral consciousness is the lived experience of *concretization*, that is, an awareness that the previous structures are very much *alive*, though latent, in the present. As William Faulkner remarked in *Requiem for a Nun*, "the past is never dead, it's not even past."

Gebser's structures offer us a broad picture of humanity: from the event horizon of hominization in the *archaic*, to the vitalist dreaming and interweaving of Paleolithic cave paintings of Chauvet and Lascaux

5   Structuralism is a school of thinking in the social sciences characterized by anthropologists such as Claude Lévi-Strauss or psychologists such as Jacques Lacan. It has since has gone out of favor in the late twentieth century after the reconstructive wave of French intellectuals such as Michel Foucault and Jacques Derrida. Typical for Gebser, his structures of consciousness defy easy categorization. His methodology—a phenomenology of consciousness centered on an initial intuition of the aperspectival—can relate both to structuralists and post-structuralist thinkers.

in the *magic*, to Chartres Cathedral and the celestial, ensouled cosmology of the *mythic*, still more to the emerging spatial and measurable waking world of the *mental*. Notice, however, how the dreaming mind and the waking mind are neither inferior nor superior to each other; rather, they are co-constituents of a larger reality. The integral, for Gebser, is likened to *clarity*. Diaphaneity. It belongs neither to the daylight nor twilight mind but instead achieves a lucid *seeing through* of these worlds as they reflect inexhaustible aspects of the Real,[6] the spiritual Origin.

What is *origin* for Gebser? The German word *Ursprung*, as the late scholar of yoga and Gebserian biographer Georg Feuerstein notes, literally means "primal leap."[7] Gebser is at times elusive here, attempting to avoid both symbolically mythical *or* precise, rational language (it is neither the mythic-tied image of a "primordial spark," nor the mental, Hegelian "being"[8]). Origin is not time-bound, nor space-bound, but is the *originator* or source of all that is time and space bound.

---

6 See J.F. Martel's *Reclaiming Art in the Age of Artifice: A Treatise, Critique and Call to Action* (Berkeley: Evolver Editions, 2015), Chapter 2.

7 Feuerstein, *Structures of Consciousness*, 45.

8 Ibid., 43.

"We might say it is sheer presence," Feuerstein writes.[9] Gebser has also described origin as "the itself," or "that which pervades or 'shines through' everything."[10] Feuerstein finds its correspondence in the "super-consciousness" of Hinduism. "For the enlightened beings of Hinduism, the *atman*, which can correctly be rendered as 'itself,' is flawless consciousness or the 'witness'... according to their testimony this witness is utterly unqualified, transpersonal, absolute."[11] The integral, then, is an actualization of this originary presence in human consciousness—a coming to awareness, an *awaring*— and the integration of all previous structures. We might also note that consciousness, for Gebser, is the capacity in human beings to integrate these structures, which ultimately falls not upon the synthesizing capacities of the mental to do so, but the originary spiritual presence—hence the need for an intensification of *presence* as precursor to their integration and realization.

---

9   Ibid., 42. "In the integral structure of consciousness this fact becomes self-evident: the originary presence is "presentiated" (*vergegenwartigt*). And this presentation of the spiritual origin enables the human being to transcend the potential exclusivity of all structures of consciousness."

10   Jean Gebser, *The Ever-Present Origin*, trans. Noel Barstad with Algis Mickunas, (Athens, OH: University of Ohio Press, 1997), 135. Hereafter EPO.

11   Feuerstein, *Structures of Consciousness*, 43.

The Integral Milieu

Readers of *Ever-Present Origin* will immediately sense great care given for the aesthetic particulars in specific works of art: a Paleolithic mask without a mouth and what we can glean from it about the auditory surround of the magical structure, for instance, or how a Minoan fresco speaks volumes about the emergence of the soul, or even how the dimension of time becomes realized in a Picasso painting. This attention to detail is at least partly credited to Gebser's own biographical context. The latter of which was not merely incidental: he was, in fact, friends with Pablo Picasso, and many other luminaries of the time. These included Federico Garcia Lorca, and Werner Heisenberg as well as religious scholars and psychologists such as C. G. Jung, Lama Anagarika Govinda, and Daisetsu Teitaro Suzuki (the latter of whom would confirm Gebser's satori experience at Sarnath, India, which we will mention at greater length later on in this volume) and frequented the famous Eranos lectures in Switzerland. It is through this correspondence and these scholarly acquaintances that Gebser first proposed the "three European worlds" of the *unperspectival*, *perspectival*, and *aperspectival* in his writing prior to *Ever-Present Origin*, in *The Grammatical Mirror*. These three worlds offer a broader overview of the coming to awareness of space and time, and to which the structures can offer us more concrete detail. Think, for instance, about the transformation from *unperspectival* medieval iconography to *perspectival* realism in Renaissance painting (to be detailed further in the following chapters). Additionally, Gebser would later come to discover and describe the "pre-eminent" works of Teilhard and Aurobindo, noting their independent corroboration of the new consciousness. Both Aurobindo's work and his own[12] would use the term "integral," though Aurobindo would describe this new consciousness particularly as the *supramental.* So, we have what might be described as *an emergent integral milieu* coming out of the mid-twentieth century.[13]

In 1985 and twelve years after Gebser's death, *Ever-Present Origin* received an English translation through communications professors Algis Mickunas

12 Gebser, *EPO*, xxix. For Aurobindo, it is the *supramental consciousness* that is being achieved by humanity, but he also described this spiritual work as *integral yoga*. Gebser also notes that Teilhard approaches this new consciousness from a "Catholic position."

13 And further still, Haridas Chaudhuri, a student of Sri Aurobindo's, helped to found and serve as the first president of the California Institute of Integral Studies (formerly the American Academy of Asian Studies), which continues to further the mission of an integral pedagogy and has gone on to catalyze the founding of the Esalen Institute (Michael Murphy drew deep spiritual inspira-

and Noel Barstad and reached the extended consciousness culture of the United States. Ken Wilber,
a Colorado-based philosopher has helped to re-ener-
gize—and tremendously popularize—the philosophy
of integral and has even adopted Gebser's terminology
(magic, mythic, mental, etc.) for his own Integral Theory in texts such as *Up from Eden*, *The Atman Project*,
and *Sex, Ecology, and Spirituality*. Yet, what is arguably
unique to Gebser in all of this is his singularly *phenomenological* approach to integral consciousness and the
structures—it is *not* developmental. Nor is it a work of
sophisticated meta-theoretical abstraction.[14] In fact,
throughout most of *Ever-Present Origin*, Gebser will
repeatedly attempt to get *out* from under the natural
machinations of the categorical mind. Much of con-

tion from Sri Aurobindo in the classic human potential movement
text *The Future of the Body*, 1992).

14 This has been a signature "trademark" of recent contemporary
discussion on models of consciousness, and to which I am sympathetic, at events such as MetaIntegral's 2013 Integral Theory Conference, where the works of philosopher Roy Bhaskar, Ken Wilber,
and Edgar Morin were synthesized into a "Meta Integral" framework. Meta-thinking, in general, is symptomatic of a hyper-syn-
thesis and theoretical integration. While useful, and interesting
at times, Gebser's approach is *not* a theory about theories, nor is
it looking to see how different theories fit together. His work de-
parts from synthesis and therefore looks not to the theories, but
the theoreticians; Gebser looks at the phenomenology of the map-
maker, with their mode of being in the world, rather than attempt-

temporary integral studies has, like the larger human potential movement and fields such as transpersonal psychology, relied predominantly on the stage-centered maps of meta-theoretical and psycho-social development to make their case for a new consciousness (with meta-thinking placed at the higher levels of these same models). While I respect these contemporary approaches and intuit they are vastly helpful in personal, therapeutic, and sometimes organizational settings, I sense they are still *other* modes of expressing the complexities of cultural evolution without becoming laden with what Gebser would describe as the problems of the late phase of the mental structure (the *mental-rational*): a spatially fixated consciousness, quantifying its flows, ultimately pinning down living reality into singular, totalizing maps. Something more like a phenomenological approach is needed, an approach likened to what William Irwin Thompson and mathematician Ralph Abraham describe as a "complex-dynamical mentality," or Gebser's own *aperspectival*. That is, a form of thinking that is process-oriented, descriptive, inhabiting unbroken flows of *becomings*

---

ing to unify any of the maps. The latter are not taken for granted as givens, and in reality are a product of a particular structure of consciousness. After all, the very word *theory* denotes a form of *seeing* and therefore invokes the mental, perspectival world.

rather than segmented and linear (or even *multi*-linear) striations. Gebser's methodology lies somewhere adjacent to—or between—rather than against meta-theoretical approaches such as Integral Theory, moving us from critique and response to alterity, seeking *new* expressions, *new statements* in the field of contemporary integral scholarship. As Octavia Butler said, "there are new suns."[15]

The time has come to retrieve Gebser's integral aperspectivity for the challenges we face in the twenty first century. It bears repeating that Gebser's time is our time. He recognized a crisis in civilization, and in the decades that have followed him, this crisis has only further compounded itself. "Such a reaction, the reaction of a mentality headed for a fall," Gebser writes at the outset of *Ever-Present Origin*, "is only too typical of man in transition."[16] This echoes our own anxieties at the end of the age of fossil fuels and at the beginning of a centuries-long epoch facing the planetary consequences of climate change. We must bear witness to the possibil-

---

15 Gerry Canavan, "'There's Nothing New / Under The Sun, / But There Are New Suns': Recovering Octavia E. Butler's Lost Parables," *Los Angeles Review of Books*: https://lareviewofbooks.org/article/theres-nothing-new-sun-new-suns-recovering-octavia-e-butlers-lost-parables/ [last accessed 10 Nov 2018].

16 Gebser, *EPO*, 1.

ity of *both* our undoing *and* our becoming if we are to truly apprehend our era. If the integral milieu—which promises a new tomorrow—is to bear any weight, to *speak* to this age of transition, it must do this *with* us.

As I hope to make clear, an integral aperspectival approach is one in which we have more room to dialogue with the developments of postmodern philosophers such as Gilles Deleuze and Félix Guattari; to concretize the *durationalism* (the philosophy of time) of Henri Bergson; to *see through* the late mental structures's machinations in runaway late-capitalism; to perceive the Janus-Faced, chaos-dynamical systems of Teilhard's planetization; or even to understand the transformations in the humanities through the transparency of objects in object-oriented ontologies (OOO), or dark ecologies, with contemporary philosophers Graham Harman and Timothy Morton.

Gebser's time, I believe, has come yet again: to help us in this age of existential and ecological crisis to think towards a planetary future.[17]

Or, we might better say: to help us recognize how the future is already thinking *us*.

17 The integral aperspectival approach is also convergent with the Integral Yoga of Sri Aurobindo; particularly in the notion of the

Time-Freedom, or the Aperspectival Becoming

An *integral* expression of emergence, evolution, and transformation without a linear or even a *multi*-linear map challenges us to seek openings, trace lines of flight into the new. Borrowing a word from Deleuze, we must *deterritorialize* our forms of thinking and expression, free ourselves from an ossified mental structure of consciousness that is *not* up to the task of *apperceiving* the whole. These new statements must be working towards an aperspectival expression in the *multiple*, dislodged from siren songs of *enframing*[18] meta narratives or clever synthesis (indeed, "generalist" forms of thinking are difficult to achieve without succumbing to this tendency, and we moderns are always

---

supramental. See Debashish Banerji's *Seven Quartets of Becoming: A Transformative Yoga Psychology Based on the Diaries of Sri Aurobindo* (2012) for an exploration of Deleuze's plane of immanence and integral consciousness.

18 See Martin Heidegger's 1954 essay, "The Question Concerning Technology." This essay posits that the way we moderns view the world is one of a violent "enframing" of nature, "challenging forth" the resources we demand from it in a "standing reserve." But this form of thinking actually removes us from an encounter with the world—we see it as one might see a supermarket; stocked shelves. The Real eludes us. This is pitted against a poesis, a creative act with the world to allow the world to reveal an aspect of itself to us—though no object can ever be totally revealed to us. Occlusion is always happening.

vulnerable to them). Such approaches can only fail to master the world because they have failed themselves. The world cannot be mastered, at any rate, with the rational mind; it must be allowed to be *wared*.

Firsthand witness to some of the atrocities of twentieth-century Europe, Gebser was understandably critical of grand narratives centered around positivist rationalizations of progress (I suspect that he would be no fan of Steven Pinker's "better angels").[19] As Deleuze writes, "it is not the slumber of reason that engenders monsters, but vigilante and insomniac rationality."[20] Yet, Gebser's deep spiritual insight—that one *could* see the span and history of consciousness doing *something*—prevented him from succumbing entirely to the deconstructive milieu of post-war Europe. Gebser intuited the postmodern era, with its tendency toward intellectual fragmentation, in his understanding that the mental consciousness was now in its ailing and late deficient form of the mental-rational (*ratio*, of course, meaning *to divide*). Indeed, the Cold War had ushered in

---

19 John Gray, "Steven Pinker is wrong about violence and war," *The Guardian*: https://www.theguardian.com/books/2015/mar/13/ john-gray-steven-pinker-wrong-violence-war-declining [last accessed 15 Nov 2018].

20 Gilles Deleuze and Félix Guattari, *Anti-Oedipus: Capitalism and Schizophrenia* (Minneapolis: University of Minnesota Press, 1983), 70.

the Atomic Age, and the dropping of the first nuclear bombs on Hiroshima and Nagasaki exhibited the devastating reality and utter dissolution of the spatial, atomized mental world itself.

What was left for Gebser to do, then, was to lean into the future and attempt to speak for it.

This is the form of integrality which must be expressed: if the mental world hinges upon the realization of space, the integral aperspectival world is endeavoring to realize *time* in its manifold forms—the breaking forth of time, sidereal time, timelessness, duration, clock time, rhythmic time, and so on into the apprehension that *time is synonymous with Origin.* Time is time-freedom. And how could this be? The ever-present origin is not divided *from* becoming, from time forms, but produces them and substantiates them, is radically immanent *to* them. "We are shaped not only by today and yesterday, but by tomorrow as well," Gebser writes.[21] The dead speak and so do our children's children—both are latent in us. Past and future loom large in the present. "Origin is ever-present... It is ever-originating, an achievement of full integration and continuous renewal."[22] And what would it

21 Gebser, *EPO,* 7.
22 Ibid, xxvii.

be to live like this? To realize it in some capacity in ourselves? This realization of time-freedom parallels the endeavor of the integral human: ego-freedom. These statements do not imply a rejection of time, nor of ego. These must remain. Suffused through in a *diaphaneity*, they cease to become fixities and transform into openings and expanses. Only an *integral* human being, one who has *wared* the whole, is capable of overcoming their own fragmentation and leaping from planetary crisis to planetary consciousness. This is our individual and collective task.

The integral aperspectival approach—of which there is no *one*, totalizing, or orienting approach, because it *opens*—responds to fixation by irruption, undoes rigidification by release (rather than mere *fracturing* or ratio), liberates constricted self-sense into the abyss. Yet the terror of the abyss is also a sky—the luminous void—for the integral human being. *The aperspectival is immanent, and therefore finds itself at home with the philosophy of the future*: the networks of the distributed planetization to come. The integral is friendly to the concept of the rhizome in Deleuze and Guattari's *A Thousand Plateaus*: immanental, the aperspectival rhizome is inexhaustible, and so it springs forth, abolishing the limits of near and far, yesterday and tomorrow, yet creatively fulfilling them, actualizing the needs of the present without becoming frozen in clock-time's segmentation. This is what might be called an integral futurism (this is not Gebser's terminology but my own). An integral futurism is liberated from a deficient mental-rational futurism, which can only be time-bound, captured by perspectival linearity, and must achieve great speed and complexity in an attempt to escape, to *master*, the time factor. This is expressed in the *dromological* image of Paul Virilio's speeding vector, a vehicle zipping into the perspectival horizon; think of the iconic motorcycle chase in Katsuhiro Otomo's 1988 film *Akira*. An integral futurism is a speaking *from* the aperspectival realization of time wholeness; it must be suffused with a recognition of the multidimensional approach, one in which tomorrow is not mere fantasy or projection but a tangible *latency*.

The future must still be spoken for, and so in our time which we now call the Anthropocene—where human beings have an impact on the geological record of deep time with our fossil fuels—we are undoing civilization and in our dissolution becoming something else. We are what eco-philosopher Tim Morton describes as a "hyper-object," entangled in a web of interrelations between the sum total of human activities and the climate of planet Earth.[23] The human is becoming non-human; cities becoming one with the storms that bear down upon them. Distinctions melt down in the dawning of Teilhard's planetization.

This is the aperspectival world Gebser warned us about. The new mutation—tomorrow—is already here.

23 See Timothy Morton's *Hyperobjects: Philosophy and Ecology after the End of the World* (Minneapolis: University of Minnesota Press, 2013), 128. "The historic moment at which hyperobjects become visible by humans has arrived. This visibility changes everything... This is a momentous era, at which we achieve what has sometimes been called *ecological awareness*... a detailed and increasing sense, in science and outside of it, of the innumerable interrelationships among lifeforms and between life and non-life... What it means is that the more we know about the interconnection, the more it becomes impossible to posit some entity existing beyond or behind the interrelated beings." It becomes clear, as one reads Gebser, that Morton's hyperobject is an aperspectival concept.

2

A Catalytic Reading

TO SUM UP *The Ever-Present Origin* in a short volume is no easy task. It can only be a distillation—a tincture—of the much larger text. This book may also assist the reader who is unsure what to make of the dense, meticulous, and Germanic style that embodies much of Gebser's writing. To parse the whole, as it were. Although capable at times of profoundly poetic and spiritual expression, the book is not easy to digest (nor, arguably, is it meant to be). Indeed, it might be argued that *The Ever-Present Origin* is intended to produce a direct *encounter* in the reader. As I have discussed with other Gebserian scholars, it is the kind of book that exemplifies a form of *catalytic literature*, or a *literary psychoactive* par-excellence: a reading that provokes an intensified state of awareness in the reader.[1]

---

1   A number of books that function as textual singularities do this in popular culture, and do it well. In recent years we might describe a similar type of catalytic reading happening through C. G. Jung's *The Red Book* (2009) or Philip K. Dick's *The Exegesis* (2011).

The key, I think, is a reading that *provokes*; a move from an observer of distant mental categories to *participant* in lived realities. This vulnerability to the text provides an opening, a space, to *concretize* the structures within us. "To be sure," Gebser writes, "this requires co-operation; for this reason the book itself has been written in such a way as to require a certain participation of the reader."[2] Gebser's structures, like Jung's "reality of the psyche," should *stir* something in you. You find something there, already present, and at last recognized.

Forever is Gebser pointing out in his work the *non*-conceptual, or should we say *a*-rational, *waring* of origin: "We partake every moment of our lives in the originary powers of an ultimately spiritual nature," he writes.[3]

It is my hope that the following chapters provide a fair summary and introduction to the major concepts in Gebser's work—*the unperspectival, perspectival, and aperspectival worlds*—and a good understanding of the process through which the structures of consciousness become realized *in* us.

2 Gebser, *EPO*, 278.

3 Ibid.

3

A Few Words on Approach,
Or
How to Render the Invisible,
Visible

I N THE GENERATIONAL GAP between the mid-century, when Gebser was writing, and the twenty-first century, we have had the advent of Marshall McLuhan's electronic culture, the rise and fall of television, the birth of the internet (which, too, has moved from the utopian WELL (Whole Earth 'Lectronic Link) to the panopticon capitalism of Mark Zuckerburg's Facebook), and the post 9/11 world. Neo-liberalism, late capitalism, and the devastation wrought by changing climate mark the undoing of a mode of consciousness and collective action that has already long outlived itself.

The present moment oscillates between the allure of the new (the integral world) to *break forth* and the old (the mental world) to *persist*, and therefore, in that

Janus-faced place, produces a catastrophe—a word which literally means "overturning"—of consciousness. In the interim age, we both fail *and* succeed to rise to planetization. This insight is frustrating for those who hold onto hopes for that long-awaited literalized transformation (the ever-nearing eschatological New Age), but for the scholar of consciousness evolution, the process is never linear, *nor* singular. It is therefore not a localized "event."

To paraphrase the character Dr. Ford in the recent HBO series *Westworld*: the evolution of consciousness is not a ladder, but a *labyrinth*. And the processes through which cultural evolution occurs are often invisible, distributed across disparate networks of climactic events, generational drift, new artistic sensibilities, and life-world transitions. To really *see* these cultural transformations occurring, as McLuhan often notes, we need to render them visible through art.[1] William Irwin Thompson also helps us to understand this point when he discusses how the leap from one epoch to another is never experienced as a literal *event*, but as a *myth*:

1   Marshall McLuhan, *Understanding Media: The Extensions of Man* (Cambridge, MA: MIT Press, 1994).

A horizon provides an edge to our experience; if we move closer to it, it moves away, for it is not the content of our experience but the structure of our knowing. And so it is with myth and history. Myth is the horizon of history, in its modality as the past, it is the world of legend; in its modality as the future, it is the world of prophecy and science fiction. If we try to move into this horizon bodily, to rent a flat in Atlantis or freeze our bodies for later regeneration in some future-perfect science in which death will have been conquered, we try to move into the horizon and eliminate the sky to make it as prosaic, literal, and three-dimensional as the ego. This form of psychic fundamentalism flattens out experience to crush the multidimensionality of the universe... Precisely because consciousness is multidimensional, we need horizons, for there is always more "going on" with us than what takes place in historical events or personal conversations.[2]

Gebser provides us with similar insight. He described his own approach as *Kulturphilosophie* ("Cultural Philosophy"), a "method and art," and so an approach to

2   William Irwin Thompson, *Pacific Shift* (San Francisco: Sierra Club, 1985), 16.

the evolution of consciousness that works *with* specific acts of creation—be they myths, stone carvings, surrealist paintings, or even scientific theories—is working towards an insight into the phenomenology of those lifeworlds, an insight into the structures from which they were inscribed. Gebser's structures of consciousness, like McLuhan's media ecologies and Thompson's myth, helps us to *see through* culture and render visible those invisible workings that lie underneath the surface of aesthetic and historical forms. As Gebser writes, *Kulturphilosophie*'s intention is to "appraise the multiplicity of cultural endeavors."[3]

Cultural transformation *is* occurring, although we cannot always pin down those precise moments of when and where (there will be a few notable exceptions). Cultural evolution is really more like the hyper-objects of Tim Morton: strangely large and extended over time and space. Events like climate change or industrial pollution or even dark matter—"dark ecology"[4] for that matter—are all too real. As real as you and I. We meet the hyper-object called climate change when we stockpile water for abnormally strong hurricanes or avoid

3   Feuerstein, *Structures of Consciousness*, 192. Translation.

4   Timothy Morton, *Dark Ecology: For a Logic of Future Coexistence* (New York: Columbia UP, 2016).

red tide on the beaches, or flee whole towns and cities as wildfires sweep across our previously safe homes and suburbs. It is here, and *present* (uncomfortably and tragically so in these cases), albeit in a different way. This is a new kind of seeing. And so, too, do the structures exist in a kind of liminal space, superseding the merely mental category of being "here" or "there," but not necessarily precluding that, either.

Before we proceed, it is worth noting one more crucial point: *Gebser's cultural phenomenology predominantly focuses on the history of consciousness in Western civilization* (and, to a limited extent, the Mediterranean region). We can attribute this Eurocentrism to the limited availability of knowledge in his time (mid-century) and writing, as Thompson notes, during war-torn Europe.[5] Gebser's *later* writings (post *Ever-Present Origin*) would more fairly explore Asian cultures and enter into dialogue with scholars such as Govinda or Suzuki.

This volume follows Gebser's footsteps and primarily focuses on what he documents in his magnum opus; it works to summarize the text's central concepts and highlight the most potent illustrations of the structures. I will also occasionally constellate recent media examples and show how the structures continue

5   William Irwin Thompson, *Coming Into Being*, 12.

to be relevant in and for our contemporary world (this actually deserves its own volume).

It is my hope that readers, especially consciousness scholars, see my treatment of Gebser's work on the phenomenology of consciousness and his cultural philosophy as an opportunity to bring the structures into dialogue with their own findings and from their own histories. Any work that must be done in furthering a more integral tomorrow is surely through the collaboration of planetary artists, scholars, and philosophers.

To know the future, however, we must study the past, and so we turn now to a study of the "three worlds": the unperspectival, perspectival, and aperspectival.

"Clearly discernible worlds stand out whose development or unfolding took place in mutations of consciousness."
—Gebser, *EPO*, 1.

"The aperspective consciousness structure is a consciousness of the whole, an integral consciousness encompassing all time and embracing man's distant past and his approaching future as a living present."
—Gebser, *EPO*, 6

4

Three Worlds

Coming to Awareness

"**M**AN'S COMING TO AWARENESS," Gebser remarks at the very outset of *Ever-Present Origin*, "is inseparably bound to his consciousness of space and time."[1] It is from here that the structures of consciousness follow. This phenomenological approach, one in which we consider the "consciousness of space and time" in any epoch "through unique forms of visual as well as linguistic expression,"[2] is where we derive the designations of *unperspectival*, *perspectival*, and *aperspectival*. In this chapter, we will move in an admittedly chronological fashion through these broad phenomenological views before exploring the more qualitatively discrete structures: the archaic, magic, mythic, mental, and integral mutations.

1 Gebser, *EPO*, 2.
2 Ibid.

At the outset, know that the challenge here is not to settle with intellectual synthesis. Gebser clarifies his terminology when he tells us that the aperspectival is not the antithesis of perspectival (that would be the unperspectival) world. We can only note briefly here that a synthesis would mean little more than a perspectival-rational, that is, a *mental* activity, and as such would only be a temporary solution. Rather, the *a* in aperspectival is intended to denote its *liberational* quality, an overcoming of the "mere antithesis of affirmation and negation."[3] Throughout Gebser's work, the prefix *a*- stands in for freedom in all its qualities of manifestation (*a*rational, *a*perspectival, *a*mensional), a freedom *from* and *for* the boundless world.

The structures of consciousness express the emergence and coming to consciousness of the human species (and we may even want to push that back further, *much, much* further). While Gebser was concerned with the contemporary struggle to realize a new, aperspectival world, integral to the understanding of the new is an intensified awareness, and integration, of the latent old.

Most important of all: integrality, aperspectivity, is the recognition of the "powers" behind the realization

3 Ibid.

of these structures of consciousness. That is, our spiritual origin.

So we begin with the three worlds and then, to further concretize them, move into the details of the four mutations.

The Unperspectival World, or the Dreaming Vault of Stars

In the unperspectival world, space—as in the measurable, objective space conceived of in modernity— lies dormant. This is the world of the archaic, magic, and mythic structures respectively, although we will discuss those soon in greater detail. Identity in this world is still *with* the cosmos, in what Owen Barfield, another scholar of the evolution of consciousness, described as a state of *original participation*.[4] Here the self has yet to differentiate, to stand *apart* from the world, and so the communal consciousness of self-and-world, self-and-animal, self-and-tribe, and self-and-spirits is continuous and predominant. Space exists, but only as *enclosure*—vaulted and cavernous, or else as a relational nexus (space as liminality).

4 See Owen Barfield, *Saving the Appearances* (Hanover: University Press of New England, 1988).

One experiential method for us to reengage this mode of consciousness is to watch Werner Herzog's 2010 documentary, *Cave of Forgotten Dreams* (preferably in a darkly lit room with good acoustics). Approximately 30,000 years old and located in southern France, the paintings of Chauvet cave reveal some of the oldest known human art. Chauvet rivals the great works of any modernist achievement such as Michelangelo's Sistine Chapel or even the equally famous Paleolithic site of Lascaux. Herzog's orchestral soundtrack presents the cave as if it were a kind of primordial cathedral. Lions, horses, cave bears, wooly mammoths, and rhinos—these animals, multi-limbed like Shiva, dance on the cave wall. They imply movement when viewed as intended through the flickering of ancient torchlight. "Man's lack of spatial awareness is attended by a lack of ego-consciousness," Gebser writes, "since in order to objectify and qualify space, a self-conscious 'I' is required that is able to stand opposite or confront space."[5] Gebser also speaks of unperspectival space as an "enclosure in the world, an intimate bond between outer and inner."[6] This world is an enchanted one, haunted by a diffuse subjectivity and the transparen-

5 Gebser, *EPO*, 10.
6 Ibid.

cy of the human being to the presence of the numinous Other (this is our first and longest standing structure of consciousness, it could be argued, one which we have inhabited for over 100,000 years: the consciousness of animism).

Inner and outer, subject and object, are permeable membranes for the unperspectival self. Historian Richard Tarnas describes this world as one in which, "the human psyche is embedded within a world psyche in which it completely participates and by which it is continuously defined."[7] The subject-object rupture between self and world would come later, and through the evolutionary drift of human civilization, continue to widen the gap between human beings and their participation in an ensouled cosmos. The gravity of this rupture cannot be understated. Tarnas continues:

> By the late modern period, the cosmos has metamorphosed into a mindless, soulless vacuum, within which the human being is incongruently self-aware. The Anima Mundi has dissolved and disappeared, and all psychological and spiritual qualities are now located exclusively in the human mind and psyche.

7 Richard Tarnas, *Cosmos and Psyche* (New York: Penguin, 2006), 17.

...The forging of the self and the disenchant-
ment of the world, the differentiation of the human and the appropriation of meaning, are all aspects of the same development. In effect, to sum
up a very complex process, the achievement of
human autonomy has been paid for by the experience of human alienation.[8]

It may be, however, that such a rupture—into alienation and autonomy—is itself a part of the larger integral process of coming to wholeness. As Gebser writes,
"only distanciation contains the possibility for the
awakening of consciousness."[9]

The unperspectival world, the *world-as-cave*, does
not come to an end in the Paleolithic.[10] Gebser traces
it up and through to the vaulted chambers of Ancient
Egyptian architecture, the Euclidian intercolumnar
spaces of Hellenistic Greece in the Parthenon, and
further into the European Middle Ages in the "gilt
ground" (gold plated) Romanesque artwork and their
Biblical iconography (not to mention the cavernous

8   Ibid., 25.

9   Gebser, *EPO*, 542.

10   John David Ebert, *The New Media Invasion: Digital Technologies and
     the World They Unmake* (Jefferson: McFarrland, 2011), 23. Ebert
     refers to the unperspectival world as the "world as cavern."

architecture of cathedrals themselves). These *flat* paintings of angels and saints are lacking perspectival depth. The sky, when it is depicted, is a not an open sky, but a vaulted starry cavern.

If we depart from medieval Europe for a moment and examine some of the more contemporary archeological findings since Gebser's writing, we find that the Paleolithic cave is recreated in some of the earliest human settlements. In the Neolithic city of Catal Huyuk, inhabited approximately around 7500 BCE and located in southern Anatolia (modern day Turkey), domiciles were accessible *only* through their roofs. Interior walls were decorated with Paleolithic motifs of the goddess, the bull, and the hunt. The dead—the ancestors— were never far away from the living as they were often buried beneath the family's sleeping chambers;[11] this, again, linking the dreaming and the dead, the womb of the Earth and the afterlife,[12] the visible and invisible, in a single continuum.

All of these examples are intended to demonstrate the *dreamlike* quality of the unperspectival world to

11 See Michael Balter, *The Goddess and the Bull: Catalhoyuk: An Ar-chaeological Journey to the Dawn of Civilization* (New York: Free Press, 2006).

12 See William Irwin Thompson, *Self and Society: Studies in the Evolution of Culture* (Exeter: Imprint Academic, 2009), 9.

the reader. Space exists, but not in any way we moderns can readily conceive: it is the dream space, a symbolic space, where starry signifiers carry the primordial language of the cosmos. The whole world *speaks*. This is a celestial consciousness, and also where Gebser's magical structure comes into play: all things relate to all other things. All things correspond. And, since the whole world is speaking for the magical individual, they must listen intently. The world-as-cave, like traveling into the actual caves of Chauvet or Lascaux, is an acoustic experience. Bellowing voices—of the living, the dead, and other-than-human—sound in the dark.

It is no wonder that the vault and the column are so prevalent. As a recent discovery suggests Neanderthals, approximately 200,000 years ago, were building ritualistic spaces in the deep caves of southwest France. Stalagmite was heated by flame, then split open—demonstrating sophistication of technique—and arranged in interlinking circles with the bones of animals.[13] The imprint of this enclosed space—this world-as-cave—is as much linked to the heavens as it is to the cavernous depths: the enclosure of the world

---

13 Ian Sample, "Neanderthals Built Mysterious Cave Structures 175,000 Years Ago," *The Guardian*: https://www.theguardian.com/science/2016/may/25/neanderthals-built-mysterious-cave-structures-175000-years-ago [last accessed 21 Dec 2018]

for the unperspectival self is, in reality, the opening of another. A world of psychic participation. With megalithic structures built around the planet corresponding to sophisticated astronomical knowledge and predating civilization (Gobekli Tepe is the most startling example, and Gordon White's *Star.Ships* explores this in depth), we know that the unperspectival consciousness was as challengingly complex as our own. We also know that the closing down of this participatory cosmos was as much a terrific gain as it was a terrible loss.

The vault and the column, notably present in the megalithic structures found virtually around the world called dolmens, are important for Gebser as they engendered a kind of procreative tension in unperspectival consciousness—the phallic male column and the feminine cave-as-womb (the perspectival world, in other words, is a *latent* within the unperspectival). This tension, Gebser suggests, is brought together in the architecture of Christianity, whose image of Christ foreshadowed the coming individuation process. Christ is the figure "who will create his own space,"[14] and announce the coming emergence of the modern ego.[15] Gebser suggests that it was the European

---

14 Gebser, *EPO*, 11.

15 We might also add the Egyptian myth of Isis and Osiris here. Isis,

Renaissance—starting around 1250 CE—that would take the incipient forms of perspective from medieval cosmology and the Hellenistic world and fully achieve them. Yet, as noted earlier, cultural evolution does not happen in a neat and linear progression. The awareness of perspective would have its earlier harbingers in the still-life paintings of Pompei, the early portraiture of Rome, the pastoral scenes in the Latin poet Virgil's *Eclogues*, or still earlier in Aristotle's approach to studying the natural world not according to its ideal, Platonic form but through discrete analysis (a kind of proto-empiricism).

The Perspectival World:
To the Eye, All That is Measurable

It was the Greeks who would harbor an early form of individuation, but only for the notable and powerful in the idealized busts of deities, emperors, and philosophers. The Renaissance period saw a more radical move in the depiction not of these larger-than-life figures, but in the portraits of everyday people. Individuation was emerging in the Netherlands through the

the divine mother, and Osiris, the father and lord of the underworld, produce Horus, who ushers in a new age.

portraiture of perspectival innovator Jan van Eyck, or through in the paintings of Giotto di Bondone, where a "new psychic awareness of space"[16] was now coming to the forefront.

Gebser mentions a number of developments in this period that helped to shape the new spatial consciousness. The troubadours usage of "I" in their lyricism (noted also by Julian Jaynes in his own theory of coming to self-consciousness in his theory of the *bicameral mind*),[17] the Catholic theologian Thomas Aquinas siding with Aristotle over Plato and thus favoring the spatial world over the "psychic bound, Platonic world."[18] The Troubadors, like Virgil's earlier works, estrange our identification with the world by defining an *I* that looks *upon* nature rather than participating *in* it. More pertinently to the theme of this book is the coming to consciousness of spatialized time. We move from the rhythmicity of unperspectival time (celestial and qualitative) to mechanical time in the building of the first public clock in Westminister Palace in 1283. Clock time had its earlier inception, too, through its origins in the

---

16 Gebser, *EPO*, 11.

17 See Julian Jaynes, *The Origins of Consciousness in the Breakdown of the Bicameral Mind* (New York: Houghton Mifflin Harcourt, 1990).

18 Gebser, *EPO*, 11.

ascetic lives of the Benedictine monks.

Perhaps one of the most powerful moments of reflection in *Ever-Present Origin* is Gebser's exegesis of Petrarch's 1336 ascent to Mount Ventoux. Petrarch, or Francesco Petrarca, is considered one of the first humanists and widely held as the initiator of the Renaissance. Writing in the style of St. Augustine's *Confessions* to his mentor, Francisco Diorigi di Borgo san Sepolero, Petrarch tells of the ascent of Mt. Ventoux with his brother. Mt. Ventoux's surrounding region was home to the troubadours and the Cathars—a "gnostic climate"—Gebser tells us. "Here, the Gnostic tradition had encouraged investigation of the world and placed greater emphasis on knowledge than belief."[19] Petrarch's interior struggle with his own predilection—standing between the world-as-cave and the stunning vistas of perspectival space—marks the discovery of landscape and the momentous leap into spatial awareness:

> When Petrarch's glance spatially isolated a part of nature from the whole, the all-encompassing attachment to sky and earth and the unquestioned, closed unperspectival ties are severed.

19 Ibid., 13.

The isolated part becomes a piece of land created by his perception. It may well be that with this event a part of the spiritual, divine formative principle of heaven and earth (and nature in its all-encompassing sense) was conveyed to man. If this is indeed so, then from that day of Petrarch's discovery outward man's responsibility was increased. Yet regarded from our vantage point, it is doubtful whether man has been adequate to this responsibility.[20]

It is worth quoting Petrarch, by way of Gebser's translation, at length:

Shaken by the unaccustomed wind and the wide freely shifting vistas, I was immediately awestruck. I look: the clouds lay beneath my feet... I look towards Italy, whither turned my soul even more than my haze, and sigh at the sight of the Italian sky which appeared more to my spirit than to my eyes, and I was overcome by an inexpressible longing to return home... Suddenly a new thought seized me, transporting me from space into time. I said to myself: it has been ten years since you left Bologna...[21]

20 Ibid.
21 Ibid., 14.

Gebser interprets Petrarch's sudden nostalgic pining for his Italian youth as a kind of reflex—a *fleeing*—from the new reality of space back into the "golden ground of the Siena masters."[22] After further gazing upon the Pyrenees mountains, the mountains of Lyon, and the Rhône, he turns to a copy of Augustine's *Confessions*. To his utter bewilderment and in a moment profound synchronicity, Petrarch opens to this passage:

> And men went forth to behold the high mountains and the mighty surge of the sea, and the broad stretches of the rivers and the inexhaustible ocean, and the paths of the stars, and so doing, lose themselves in wonderment.[23]

Richard Tarnas helps to expand upon Gebser's insight. "Petrarch was so moved by the coincidental force of Augustine's words," Tarnas writes, "that he remained silent for the entire descent down the mountain. He at once recognized the coincidence as part of a larger pattern of such transformative moments that had happened to others in the history of spiritual con-

22 Ibid.
23 Tarnas, *Cosmos and Psyche*, 52.

versions."²⁴ Like Petrarch, Augustine had his own synchronistic experience in the garden of Milan in 386 CE:

> In a frenzy of spiritual crisis, he heard a child's voice from a nearby house mysteriously repeating the words, "Tolle, lege" ("Pick up and read"). Uncertain of their significance, he finally opened at random a copy of Saint Paul's epistles and there read words that spoke with uncanny precision to the nature of his lifelong conflict and its resolution.²⁵

While for St. Augustine this synchronicity ushered in the era of Christendom for medieval Europe, Petrarch's epiphany heralded the new perspectival world of the Renaissance.²⁶ "The old world where only the soul is wonderful and worthy of contemplation... now begins to collapse," Gebser writes, "there is a gradual but increasingly evident shift from time to space until the soul wastes away in the materialism of the nineteenth

---

24 Ibid, 53.

25 Ibid.

26 Ibid. "This time the synchronistic epiphany unfolded in a new direction with difference consequences—one revelation in the garden, pointing to Christianity and the Middle Ages, the other on the mountain, pointing to the Renaissance and Modernity."

century."[27] From this moment forward, humanity is no longer *in* the world, but begins to *possess* it.

A number of important artists are mentioned at this crucial beginning: Giotto's paintings denote a "freer treatment of space and landscape," and his students, such as Fra Angelico, continue to develop a sense of perspective and realism in their art (when examining Fra Angelico's depictions of Annunciation, for instance, a notable shift in symbolic representation occurs. Figures become more realistically proportioned, there is *depth* in space, nature becomes a pleasing landscape rather than iconographically symbolized as Eden). Cennino Cennini writes the first theoretical treatise on art, and Leon Battista Alberti writes *Della pittura* in 1436 which, among many things, presents a theory of perspective in art with the visual pyramid (this work would go on to influence Leonardo Da Vinci and his posthumous *Trattato Della Pittura*). Notably, Gebser mentions the heralding Luca Pacioli's *Divina Proporzione*, which celebrated perspective as the "eighth art" (the other seven being architecture, sculpture, painting, music, poetry, dance, and performing). And here we are treated with Gebser's fine attention to language. "With the arrival of the eighth 'art'... the world

27 Gebser, *EPO*, 15.

of the ancient seven-planet heaven collapses." In other words, the world-as-cave. Negating the *n* in *Nacht* (night) for the eight, *Acht*, rouses us into the Apollonic world, the waking world, the world of daylight. "The heptagonal cosmos of the ancients and its mystery religions are left behind," Gebser writes, "and man steps forth to integrate and concretize space."[28]

This integration, however, can only be partial. Recall Gebser's comments on Petrarch's vision: the eye renders only a *segment* of the landscape. In the increasingly spatialized consciousness that would come to identify modernity, space is antithetical to totparticipation. The world withdraws its numinous qualities, its enchantment, as the self incorporates those qualities alone (meaning is merely within *us* and not out *there* in the world). The eye that renders space becomes fixed and total, but this also means that Alberti's pyramidic vision becomes a constricting prison for the Real; non-material realities, which the ancients were far more intimate with than we moderns, become further estranged from us. As we cut out the symbolic realm of a participatory cosmos, we divide ourselves.

In the perspectival consciousness, our vision expands to the cosmos in a new, measurable light, but proportionate to that opening up of space is a narrowing down of the world to the mere measurable. This is not immediate—during the fourteenth and fifteenth centuries we are still painting frescoes of Mary's Annunciation and the imagery of Christendom is still prevalent—but it is nevertheless pervasive:

> Perspectival vision and thought confine us within spatial limitations... The positive result is a concretion of man and space; the negative result is the restriction of man to a limited segment where he perceives only one sector of reality. Like Petrarch, who separated landscape from land, man separates from the whole only that part which his view or thinking can encompass, and forgets those sectors that lie adjacent, beyond, or even behind. One result is the anthropocentrism that has displaced what we might call the theocentrism previously held. Man, himself a part of the world, endows his sector of awareness with primacy; but he is, of course, only able to perceive the partial view. The sector is given prominence over the circle; the part outweighs the whole. As the whole cannot be approached from a perspectival attitude to the world, we merely superimpose the character of wholeness onto the sector,

the result being the familiar "totality."[29]

Gebser gives further cause to view the developments of modernity with profound caution. *Totus* in Latin has ambivalent etymological roots, meaning both *all* and *nothing*. Further, he notes an audible similarity between *totus* and the German *tot* ("dead").[30] The statement here is clear: totalizing orientations inflate the part for the whole. They are a kind of ersatz wholeness. The whole can only be approached by the emerging aperspectival attitude, which, even in our day, has yet to be realized in its fuller extent.

Regardless of these cautions, the spatial world was already bursting through with fervor. In the early struggle of individual artists to *realize* space within themselves—within their souls, as it were—we see another example of McLuhan's artist, who recognizes a change in the climate of consciousness and feels urged, even compelled by such a new reality to actualize and externalize it in their works. But as the Scientific Revolution nears, we see a kind of creative, synchronous and sweeping explosion of this new consciousness throughout Europe:

29 Ibid., 18.
30 Ibid.

Copernicus, for example, shatters the limits of the geocentric sky and discovers heliocentric space; Columbus goes beyond the encompassing Oceanus and discovers earth's space; Vesalius, the first major anatomist, bursts the confines of Galen's ancient doctrines of the human body and discovers the body's space; Harvey destroys the precepts of Hippocrates' humoral medicine and reveals the circulatory system. And there is Kepler, who by demonstrating the elliptical orbit of the planets, overthrows antiquity's unperspectival world-image of circulars and flat surfaces (a view still held by Copernicus) that dated back to Ptolemy's conception of the circular movement of the planets.[31]

Galileo at this time is also making breakthroughs with his discovery of Jupiter's moons (now appropriately named the Galilean moons). Regarding lenses—which are very much a technological extension of the eye—philosopher John David Ebert, in his *New Media Invasion*, recalls that Copernicus himself was a lens grinder, and that much of modernity has relied upon the organ of sight. "The achievements of natural phi-

31 Ibid., 21.

losophers like Roger Bacon, Galileo, and Descartes were made possible, to a very large degree, by their fascination with the properties of optical devices."[32] This new form of sight, not of the imaginal, psychic, or soul-bound world-spaces but the measurable spaces of the daylight, finds its correlate in the development of Johannes Gutenberg's printing press, moving literature from the illuminated manuscript to the printed book. This is McLuhan's move from scribal culture to print culture. "The light from another world shines *through* all cultural phenomena of the Medieval Era," writes Ebert on McLuhan's distinction between medieval and modernist technologies (these illuminated manuscripts required to be lit from *within*, as it were, with a candle lighting up the text from behind). But, henceforward after Gutenberg, the text no longer invokes transparency. Print media requires light to be shined *on* rather than *through*.[33]

The cave wall has burst and the light, at last, has broken in (and humanity broken *out*). But to what end?

Through the irruption of space, Empire reaches a new and ultimate extension in the colonialism of Europe's powers in the New World, the destruction

32 Ebert, *New Media Invasion*, 7.
33 Ibid, 20.

of Meso-American civilizations and the genocide of countless indigenous populations not just on Turtle Island, but the world over.

The light of reason may produce wonders, but there are also new and greater monsters indeed.

Fractured Spectacle and the Guilt of the Time

The perspectival world is home for Gebser's mental structure of consciousness, where the eye is dominant—simultaneously opening *and* closing down worlds through the totalizing sight of sectored perspectives, each one universalizing their point of view—and we can see this evolve all the way into our contemporary technological moment. Podcaster, artist, and researcher on consciousness studies Michael Garfield has appropriately described the modern era, starting with the Scientific Revolution, as the "Glass Age."[34] The optics of the early modernists has transubstantiated into the looking glass of smart phones and tablets. We gaze out from our virtually mediated selves, and our vision splinters like a thousand fragments of glass.

---

34 See Phil Ford, J.F. Martel, and Michael Garfield. "Living in a Glass Age, with Michael Garfield," *Weird Studies*, https://www.weird-studies.com/26 [last accessed 1 Dec 2018].

Who can we see with this form of vision? Can the others, the Other, see truly see us this way?

Even though Gebser wrote *Ever-Present Origin* over half a century ago, he seems to have hit the mark for where we, as a culture, stand today. Since the spatial world is a fragmented world, Gebser traces the rise of colonialism, political revolution, schisms, and theological fracturing as a necessary consequence of the age of sectoring perspectivalism (another McLuhan note: recall that the printing press and the Gutenberg Bible were precursors to Martin Luther's *Ninety-Five Theses* and subsequent rise of Protestantism in Europe). These fractures are liberational insofar as they concern the gaining of *new* centers of self-determinacy. Perspectival points of view (individual rights or the construction of discrete national identities) burst and rupture from the enclosed ties of the medieval reality with its predetermined social caste. There is much work to be done in striking out into a new world. With the new world comes a new self setting out on a struggle towards self-determination, autonomy, and freedom of expression (which, for the perspectival self, is often a struggle *opposed* to or *aimed at* the object in perspectival space).

The problems of modernity are well spoken for in many contemporary writings, but here Gebser helps provide us insight with respect to the imminent aperspectival world. Having fully mastered the dimension of *space* from within themselves, *time* itself became the next venture for human consciousness. The perspectival world, however, can never master time; time, in its truest form for Gebser, is the whole, is origin. Spatialized time is an inadequate realization. Anything as partial and segmented as the hypertrophied ego whose limited view has become a totality—an ersatz wholeness—can never master time.

Time, in the late perspectival age, the age of the mental-rational structure of consciousness, manifests as *guilt*. We are forever "out of time," and time itself becomes vacuous, devoid of any inherent quality, and needing to be filled by our activities. The modernist must "kill time" and remind themselves that "time is money." The statement "I have no time" is our admittance that we possess space but not time.[35] For Gebser, this frenzied response to time is indicative of our helplessness towards the aperspectival world. Time becomes a marker of anxiety for the ego, for *Kronos devours his children*, and time becomes the counted beads in the hour glass which inevitably slip down to zero: the vanishing point for the dissolution of ego. On a perspectival plane, the event horizon is the end point for

35 Gebser, *EPO*, 22.

the eye that perceives it. If the spatial self—the waking ego—in a material world is *all* that we are, then of course we are terrified by the thought of it coming to an end. "The deeper and farther we extend our view into space, the narrower is the sector of our visual pyramid," Gebser writes, speaking of a "universal intolerance" beginning to manifest itself in the twentieth century.[36] "He "sees" only a vanishing point lost in the misty distance... and he feels obliged to defend his point fanatically, lest he lose his world entirely."[37]

Presciently, Gebser's description for Europe in the mid-twentieth century sounds as if it were speaking *directly* to our time, where our complex heterogenous society is once again being questioned—from Brexit in the UK to "build a wall" sentiments in the United States—and the corpse of ethno-nationalism is being dredged up from its historical tomb. Totalizing worldviews enframed by what we could describe as "digital perspectivalism" (aided by social media algorithms on Facebook and other sites) have enabled every individual to splinter off into their own reality, morphing the solidity of perspectival facts into a "post-truth"

36 Ibid., 23.
37 Ibid.

world.[38] This is the perspectival world's same propensity towards ratio, generating false totalities through ever splintering, ever narrowing points of view. The endgame of perspectival consciousness in its deficient phase is infinite fragmentation, and therefore the shattering of space itself (think of modern media examples that express this bursting of perspectival space such as Rick and Morty's usage of a dizzying multiverse theory). Gebser writes of a "universal intolerance" emerging in his time:

> The European of today, either as an individual or as a member of the collective, can perceive only his own sector. This is true of all spheres, the religious as well as the political, the social as well as the scientific. The rise of Protestantism fragmented religion; the ascendancy of national states divided the Christian Occidental into separate individual states; the rise of political

38 Ken Wilber adapts Jean Gebser's "aperspectival" terminology to describe the postmodern condition where all views are correct and no one is wrong, "aperspectival madness" (See Ken Wilber, *Sex, Ecology Spirituality: The Spirit of Evolution*). This is ironic, because the so-called postmodern age in many respects is merely the perspectival age wrought to its uttermost limit: the atomization of all perspectives into their own world-spaces and the utter success of ratio to divide the world up, not into organic difference, but a shattered aggregate of points of view.

parties divided the people (or the former Christian community) into political interest groups. In
the sciences, this process of segmentation led to
the contemporary state of narrow specialization
and "the great achievements" of the man with
tunnel vision. And there is no "going back"; the
ties of the past, the re-legion, are almost non-ex-
istent, having been severed, as it were, by the cut-
ting edge of the visual pyramid. As for a simple
onward progression and continuity (which has
almost taken on the character of a flight), they
lead only to further sectors of particularization
and, ultimately, to atomization. After that, what
remains, like what was left in the crater of Hiroshima, is only an amorphous dust; and it is prob-
able that at least one part of humanity will follow
this path, at least in "spirit," i.e., psychologically.[39]

If we do not have time, time certainly has *us*. The
sweeping winds of modernization, the advancement
of technological revolutions and political revolutions
alike have deemed our age to be what James Joyce in
his *Ulysses* called the "nightmare of history." The
rapid torrent of innovation and social complexity is

39 Gebser, *EPO*, 23.

expressed positively through the writings of Pierre
Teilhard de Chardin, who sees this movement as ultimately a kind of culmination of the evolution of the
biosphere: the birth of the noosphere (the thinking
layer of the Earth) in humanity and the planetization
of consciousness. While this concept of planetization
is something Gebser might agree with in spirit, the
acceleration of change and rapid industrialization of
civilization must also be acknowledged for the crisis
of consciousness that it is. Gebser describes this as the
irruption of time. Time manifests as a *force* of nature.
Helpless to control it, time manifests not as a positive
or freeing expression for the perspectival world but as
a negative, a runaway technological evolution which
Kevin Kelly, techno-philosopher, has rightly described
as "out of control."[40]

Oscillating between a powerlessness to control the
forces unleashed by the perspectival world on the one
hand, and a total self-intoxicating power on the other—between "anxiety" and "delight"—is our modern
condition. Generations after Gebser wrote about it,
this crisis has only become *more* acute. The evolution of
consciousness does not *end* here, though. For the sake

40 See Kevin Kelly, *Out of Control: The New Biology of Machines, Social
    Systems and the Economic World* (New York: Basic Books, 1994).

of the world, the dissolution of perspectival consciousness from its fixated place must, at last, occur. Solutions to our crisis cannot originate from the same perspectival thinking, which can only continue to sector and divide. We are compelled to make an integral response; only a whole-oriented consciousness can now act and itself becomes a dire necessity—a crisis and mutation.

What we are invited to realize in our time, just like the artists and scientists of the perspectival age, is the emergence of the *aperspectival world*. This is the integral mutation. "Our epoch," Gebser writes, "must find the point where the target is already latently present."[41]

If it is in us, then we are obligated to try and invoke it, presently.

The A-Perspectival World, or Time-as-Wholeness

If the unperspectival world implies the *world-as-cavern*, the perspectival world as the *world-as-space*, then the aperspectival world releases us from the estrangement of space and returns us to a participation *with* the world through *time*.

Gebser recognizes Pablo Picasso's artwork as a remarkable concretization of aperspectival time. "For

41 Gebser, *EPO*, 24.

the first time," Gebser tells us, "time itself has been incorporated into the representation."[42] Picasso's artwork is familiar to many of us today, with its somewhat disorienting implications of multidimensionality, but Gebser suggests that we should look at it more closely. Picasso's art allows us to, "take in at once glance the whole man, perceiving not just one possible aspect, but simultaneously the front the side, and the back." This *simultaneity* becomes important, for if we *only* express time in one sequence after another we are still in perspectival time. Gebser rightly points out that time-as-sequence can only ever be an *abstracted* wholeness (and therefore still perspectival). Yet, in many of Picasso's mature works—especially his portraitures—a sense of integrality and wholeness exudes from them. This is not a spatial time, but *time-as-presence* which, for Gebser, is the radiant "quintessence of time."[43]

Before moving ahead into the aperspectival world, we can, as Gebser does in *Ever-Present Origin*, pause before leaping ahead. One of the early difficulties for the aperspectival world is what we might call *time-as-flood* (time is linked with the psyche, the past, and the image of water is often associated with the psyche).

42 Ibid.
43 Ibid., 25.

Gebser describes it as an "amalgamation of time... dredged up from oblivion... in bits and pieces" (in the Internet age this is again beginning to sound familiar with everything from aesthetic pastiche to the eerie presence of the past through digital remixing of music and photography).[44] With the twentieth century's profound reorientation around Sigmund Freud's unconscious, the floodgates of the psyche opened up and deconstructed the Victorian self to reveal all manner of erotic and carnal desires at play. Surrealism, Dada, and many other movements, Gebser points out, have their relation to the irruption of time through *psyche*. These movements can be seen as a counter to a stifling rationalism or materialism that had run its course in modernity, but they are *also* pointing towards the potentiality for an aperspectival integration of the perspectival and unperspectival worlds.

For Gebser, the three worlds of unperspectival, perspectival, and aperspectival were not enough clarification. He realized that a more distinguished and thorough phenomenological description of the coming-to-consciousness of humanity was necessary and evident. These are the structures of consciousness, which introduce to us the archaic, magic, mythic,

44 Ibid., 29.

mental, and integral forms of time-space expression. These structures allow the past, present, and future to *concretize* in a way that does not threaten to overwhelm us but reveal themselves in clarity.

5

Mutations, Structures, Becomings

Prologue: Animate Histories

B EFORE WE CAN DISCERN the new, we must come to know the old. By *knowing* the old I actually mean something like *re-constituting it*. As Deleuze says, it is not enough to *have* the unconscious, you must *produce it yourself in the present*.[1] Bringing up the structures from the depths of time, from latency, is a matter of animating them, *presently*, and as such must be a participatory process.

Revivification of the so-called *old* can be overwhelming, like how the new reality on Mount Ventoux was so disturbing for Petrarch. It is easy for us moderns to dismiss the world-as-cave and write off the unperspectivity as mere superstition. Gebser, for instance, notes how Renaissance artists regarded their medieval predecessors—in a tellingly perspectival way—as

---

1   Gilles Deleuze and Claire Parnet, *Dialogues* (New York: Columbia UP, 2002), 78.

having "false vision."[2] We hardly need to discuss the blatant scientism of our own day which seeks to explain away subjectivity itself (a form of final self-annihilation in the late mental structure).[3] To truly *integrate* the structures requires more than a mere distanced appreciation of their remote accomplishments. We must come into glimmerings of contact with the so-called past and chance, as it were, a meeting with the dead. To know the night you must risk stumbling in the dark.

The archaic, magic, and mythic always retain their potency in us; they are spiritually and ontologically present, challenging (and sometimes overtaking) the contemporary mental consciousness with the allurement of their alterity. The daylight mind looks with both superstition *and* temptation at the siren songs of dreaming phantasmagoria.[4]

So, it is recommended—as a practice—that the reader continue to observe their own awareness in this

2 Gebser, *EPO*, 21.

3 See Charles Tart, *The End of Materialism: How Evidence of the Paranormal is Bringing Science and Spirit Together* (Oakland: New Harbinger, 2009).

4 Think of the Greek myth of the oceanic Sirens, who lured sailors with their enchanting music into shipwrecks; this myth could be interpreted as describing the power of the sidereal and mythic consciousness, the oceanic realm of the soul, and its capacity to lure the ego into a state of trance.

process: as if they were holding the cultural "artifacts" that are about to be described in their own hands (or at the very least, in their own mind's eye). The reader should welcome any sudden receptivity, any inward stirrings, and moments of *felt-sense*, no matter how small or fleeting and no matter how often they might wish to take flight back to the perspectival world as the "right" world.

Like reading the pages of a book from *left* to *right*, we have the tendency to flee from the sidereal and the nighttime realm of psyche—and therefore the archaic, magical, and mythical structures—back into the wakeful sensibility of the secular world. This is a reaction all too typical of the mental, perspectival mind. Yet, integral *to* the integral mutation is the *displacement* of the mental consciousness from its perspectival throne. Spatial reality can no longer retain itself as the locus—and prime arbiter—of the Real.

This work, because it is work for many of us, invites an internal re-structuring.

We must make room again for the latent worlds within in our souls (indeed, for our souls themselves), lest they become ghosts in a haunted perspectival landscape. Some fashion of internal work is necessary to leave us properly open to these realities, while also, and critically, preventing us from being fully overtaken by

them. Gebser repeatedly recommends a "suprawake-
ful" clarity when studying these structures within
ourselves; to really concretize them in such a thorough
way that they lose some degree of fixity (this quality of
clarity is helped by the integral mutation). This inner
work is not unlike the struggles of the many artists and
individuals that Gebser documented so closely in the
previous discussion on the realization of perspectival
space.

As Gebser suggested with Petrarch, so too is it
true for us. This clarity and intensity of presence must
be brought out from within us, or conversely we must
bring this lucid presence into our consciousness.

The double task of the integral age is both the
re-integration of the twilight worlds and the concretization not of *space*, but *time*. To *ware* the whole and
allow that waring to shine *through* the archaic, magic,
mythic, and mental realities respectively. *Transparency*
is the quality of the integral structure that allows such
an integration to take place. As Rilke famously writes
in his poem *Archaic Torso of Apollo*, "there is no place
that does not see you. You must change your life."[5] To
do anything else, at this phase of human history, would

5   Peter Sloterdijk, *You Must Change Your Life* (Malden: Polity Press,
    2013), 21.

be to deny tomorrow its right to *be*; a planetary culture is not a culture of the modern but a culture of yesterday, today, and tomorrow too.

A careful reading of the structures of consciousness is one method we can use to assist us as we work to concretize the past and listen to the future, and so in this chapter we will go through Gebser's structures of consciousness and introduce a mutational process, just as we did the three worlds of the un-perspectival, perspectival, and a-perspectival.

Do watch out for those "stirrings."

Mutations, *or Discontinuous Transformations*

The structures cannot be pinned down into historical *events*, even if they manifest as particular works of art or through particular individuals. Gebser speaks of these structures as *spiritual* processes, first and foremost, and before anything else.[6] To merely historicize them would be then be a mere perspectival take, symptomatic of our modernist biases, and certainly insufficient to the integral task.

Many who come to Gebser's writing after working with other stage-based models of consciousness

6   Gebser, *EPO*, 37.

evolution are surprised to discover that the structures of consciousness are also *not developmental.* This will make better sense as actually move through the mutational process and get to the mental—our own predominant age out of which the integral mutation is still nascent—and dislodge ourselves from some of our perspectival biases.

Mutation denotes a discontinuous *leap* of consciousness which helps us avoid any developmental, progressive, or evolutionary connotations.[7] Of course this is not entirely true, as the word "mutation" most certainly *does* have a biological connotation (not to mention a science fiction one, which is intriguing, and which we will revisit in a positive light in the integral chapter). Gebser would also eventually come to use the word *evolution* in his later writings, perhaps as the term lost its mid-century positivist aura.[8] If the whole of the mutational process—which is the coming to awareness of consciousness—has any progressive claim, it is the coming to awareness *in* the human being *of* the spiritual origin (a realization of a present latency, or to borrow from Sri

---

7   Ibid., 38.

8   Jean Gebser and Scott Preston, "Jean Gebser and Integral Consciousness: The Inaugural Post," http://blog.gebser.net/2012/01/jean-gebser-integral-consciousness.html [last accessed 27 Dec 2018].

Aurobindo, an *involutionary* event). Yet, even this process for Gebser is not a linear one: "Origin itself comes to awareness in discontinuous mutation: consciousness mutations are completions of integration." Regarding the usage of developmental schema, Gebser comes down fairly hard on the social theories that were in his time, such as August Comte's "three-stage law" (moving from the theological, to the metaphysical, to the positivistic age), which he described in particular as, "patently perspectival-sectorial fixity." Gebser continues:

> The apparent succession of our four mutations is less a biological evolution than an "unfolding," a notion which admits the participation of a spiritual reality in mutation. Under no circumstances is this form of development to be considered "progress"; we must accept the term "progress" for what it is... "Progress" is not a positive concept, even when mindlessly construed to be one; progress is also a progression away, a distancing and withdrawal from something, namely, from origin.[9]

The structures unfold in dimensionality: from zero (archaic), to one (magic), to two (mythic), three (mental),

9 Gebser, *EPO*, 41.

and finally the fourth dimension (integral). There are two aspects to this structural unfolding. In the first, the mutational event is a gain in dimensionality. Think of the gains made by perspective. In the second, these same gains also become an "impoverishment because of the remoteness from origin."[10] The later structures, in other words, lose something: origin's spiritual presence.

If this is all we could say about the mutations, then Gebser's thinking would not be far from that of the Traditionalist viewpoint which reduces the perspectival age (and hence modernity) to merely a decline in the age of Kali Yuga (a *devolution* from a previous spiritual golden age). But Gebser speaks of the mutational process as "origin's development toward self-realization in man."[11] This allows us to understand remoteness from origin as a necessary space of diminishment, and the process of mutation as a punctuated breaking forth of creative, discontinuous space and time realizations. Linearity is discarded in Gebser's approach without the loss of emergence. Becoming is retained, but it is liberated from the mental's dialectical conception. Dialectical thinking—a triune process of thesis, antithesis, and synthesis—would only show up *later* in the

10   Ibid.
11   Ibid.

mental structure, piercing the eternal recurrence of oceanic thinking in the membrane of the mythic with the pyramidic spear of perspectival thought. As stated at the outset of this book, the mental is simply *not* an aperspectival form of statement (when we truly "grok" what the mental is in this chapter, as we have begun to in the previous chapter on the perspectival, this will hopefully solidify for the reader).

The integral itself reveals a process through which mutations appear to have their hidden, arational ordering: *systasis*. Systasis is a break from synthesis, dialetical, categorical, or systemic styles of thought entirely:

[Systasis] is the integrating dimension by which the three-dimensional spatial world, which is always a world of parts, is integrated into a whole in such a way that it can be stated. This already implies that it is not an ordering schema paralleling that of system. We must especially avoid the error of considering systasis—which is both process and effect—as that which is effected, for if we do we reduce it to a causal system. We must be aware that systasis has an effective character within every system. Systasis is not a mental concept, nor is it a mythical image (say) in the sense of Heraclitus' panta rei ("all things are in flux"), nor is it

a magic postulation of the interconnection of everything to and with everything else. And finally,
it is not integral, but integrating.[12]

Even at the level of a mental concept, systasis is not
easy to comprehend. Feuerstein writes that, "systasis,
in contrast to systematization, deals with the proper 'arrangement' of intensities (rather than quanti-
fied 'extensities')."[13] *Synairesis*, then, is the "mode" of
integral understanding marked by "completion," an
"encompassing all sides" whereby the individual perceives aperspectivally.[14] This is Picasso's multidimensional style of art, which indeed seems to concretely
express "all sides." What can be stated at this point is
that the process of consciousness mutation itself is not
dialectical or linear in the mental but discontinuous
and *synairetic*; the process by which cultural evolution
occurs is integral itself ("integral and integrating").[15]

12 Ibid, 310.

13 Feuerstein, *Structures of Consciousness*, 194.

14 Gebser, *EPO*, 312, note 5.

15 The synairetic challenge emerges in contemporary discussions:
    recent scholarship is moving away from linearity and develop-
    mental fixation typically present in theories on cultural evolution
    (despite the criticism that such a move is a move into "flatland"
    or "postmodernism," which, as a derogatory slander, only further
    demonstrates the ineffectuality of dialectical thinking to incor-

This means that our expressions of the evolution of consciousness—in the varied maps, models, and conceptual schematics in the field of consciousness studies—all inherit the challenge of not only describing emergence and becoming in an aperspectival mode but *being* integral themselves. Can emergence be expressed *without* linearity, or, rather, can a perspectival and categorical theory of consciousness evolution itself express the "quintessence of time?"[16]

Breaking through into a new reality is no easy task. These leaps of flight take risk and the possibility of failure, and so new forms of statement typically

---

porate systasis). Jorge Ferrer's work in *Revisioning Transpersonal Theory* (2001) and later in *Participation and Mystery: Transpersonal Essays in Psychology, Education, and Religion* (2017) are two good examples of this new style of aperspectival thinking. Ferrer, at the recent 2018 Integral European Conference, made reference to the 40 Foundation's World Religions Tree, which depicts the evolution of religious consciousness in an organic, multifaceted and nearly a-categorical fashion (from all sides, as it were); much like how the evolutionary tree of biological life is depicted today. Ferrer, in general, has been helping to move transpersonal psychology *away* from an interior colonization of consciousness via scientific empiricism. Jorge's thinking expresses an integral aperspectival method.

16 This begs the question: what does an aperspectival map of consciousness look like? Gebser gives us some indication in his deliberate attempts to disregard systemization and rational (as *ara*tional, but not *un*rational) linearity. This requires experimentation for contemporary integral scholars. Can theory become art, and if so, can a theory of consciousness somehow incorporate Picasso's time-free presence?

have their Janus-faced beginnings. Like the shift from mythic to mental consciousness, the nascent integral age will be full of many interesting and wonderful articulations that mix the old and the new. In this leap of thinking style from pyramidic linearity to spherical systasis, Gebser is perhaps unique as an integral thinker in that he made this jump so early (beginning with his research in the 1930s). Having a placeholder left for us in this challenge of systasis, we cannot simply fall back on earlier styles of thinking; a leap from the mental into the integral will truly be a leap *out* of our familiar world. In the *dissolution* of the deficient mental structure and the *solution* of the efficient integral, the new mutation is often a complete departure; another plateau.

Since the structures are always co-present, even in the archaic, they are always *latent*, and leap from their state of latency into an *efficient* phase of maturation (although Gebser would likely suggest to us not to take this biological language too seriously). This process of realization is often marked by an intoxicated frenzy of jubilant creative expression through new works of art, architecture, linguistic, spiritual, and symbolic innovations (as we saw in the previous chapter). When a structure has reached its creative zenith, it enters into a *deficient* phase—from a flowering forth to a withering away, or rigidification. The structure becomes ossified—a move from yin to yang—but with that ri- gidity there is also a fixation. In this deficient mode the seeds of a crisis begin to form; often the spiritual and creative effort of this mutation has exhausted itself and shifts from qualitative expression to quantitative inflation, like a dying star expanding into a red giant.

As is the case with our contemporary crisis, the structures often bring catastrophe upon themselves. When they finally collapse, they spur on new creative life worlds: new time-space realizations. The emergent structure may supersede the previous one in some re- spects (efficient where the former is deficient), but it does not necessarily mean the new structure properly integrates and carries forward what came before in a neat, progressive, or dialectical way. Nor is it necessar- ily in a *holonic* way (in the sense of nested levels of or- der). For instance: who is to say that the magic-mythic imaginal world is a *less* true or whole stage of conscious- ness relative to the emergent mental scientific world? With the gain of the spatial world there is a loss of the former enchanted and participatory cosmos. With the retrieval of a digital animism of sorts in the countercul- tural thinking of the 1990s—i.e., the "archaic revival" of Terence McKenna—or the McLuhanesque retriev- al of animism in the process of planetization, the case is not clear which world fits rightly into the other. In any case, the integral process implies that these worlds need to be reconstituted in our consciousness in a *healthy* rather than a *haunted* form; in the case of modernity it is the haunted "electromagnetic imaginary," where electronic culture revives the magical and mythical world through the backdoor of technological innovation (as well documented by Erik Davis in his 1999 work *Techgnosis*).

New worlds open up while others close down, and so this process of cultural evolution is more like the punctuated equilibrium of Stephen Jay Gould and Niles Eldridge than the developmental logic of Ken Wilber's "transcend and include." It is true that some qualities are retained in the new mutation and even depend on their predecessor's achievements (the emerging of mental ego is preceded by the self-consciousness of the mythical soul), but they depend on those achievements in only latency. The world-as-cave survives the mutational process as a ghost; the starry cave is shattered as the perspectival consciousness opens up its new reality with great conquering fervor and conviction, only to be recovered as a *hauntology*[17] of the mythic and magic in the form of the unconscious through Freud or Jung, or even in the electric magnetism of Mary

17   See Mark Fisher, *Ghosts of My Life* (Alesford: Zero Books, 2014).

Shelley's *Frankenstein: The Modern Prometheus*. In the wave of so-called postmodern thought, it was Deleuze who traced the process of thinking *back* to its "plane of immanence," its realm of magical interweaving and vitalist potency, and thereby traced the structures in reverse. "To think is always to follow the witch's flight," he writes.[18]

Because this process is not linear but one of discontinuous leaps into new plateaus of reality, integration does not necessarily follow new mutations until we reach the integral structure. It is in the aperspectival that systasis comes to the forefront as an *a*systematic ordering of the whole (*a* bears the mark of freedom, always, in Gebser's writing). Time realization (not clock time, mind you, but the achronon, time freedom) allows us to *live* in a new reality—a world from all sides—that does not rely on synthesis or categorical scaffolding to hold the structures together. Rather it is a reliance upon the non-human arranging of *systasis*, the integrating power of the infinite creative origin itself. By non-human, I am referring to the increasingly popular concept in the humanities of the "non-human

18 Gilles Deleuze, Félix Guattari, *What is Philosophy?* (New York: Columbia UP, 1994), 41.

turn."[19] This is a rather via-negativa approach, but we can suggest that it is also something of an aperspectival turn, useful for conceptualizing the limits of the perspectival world: an acknowledgement that we cannot quantify the Real in its totality, and a recognition of the Other. Increasingly we are seeing in the humanities an aperspectival quality to thinking itself and a transparency to the "world without us," a world that escapes the mental structure's totalizing grasp. This is expanded upon especially in Eugene Thacker's concept of the planetary (an interesting complementary to Gebser's arational and Teilhard's planetization) in *In the Dust of This Planet*.

What realizes the structures, what substantiates *all* time and space forms, is origin (*Ursprung*). Synairesis, then, in the human being, is an intensification of consciousness likened to an *allowing* or making room for this integration to occur (the active construction of mental synthesis is replaced by the "mutual perceiving and imparting of truth," predicated on *being* rather than doing). We participate in origin as it participates in us (indeed, all forms of time-space realization), and, insofar as we are transparent to it, we recognize the

19 See Richard Grusin, *The Non-Human Turn* (Minneapolis: University of Minnesota Press, 2015).

limitations of the perspectival world to grasp this reality. There is a Taoist quality of *undoing* here. Mental systemization need not be rejected on all accounts, but it does lose its privileged locus as the center of human activity. The perspectival world is restored to a proper relation with the unperspectival and the aperspectival. Here is where Gebser's concept of the move from philosophy (thinking about truth) to "verition" (being-in-truth), finally becomes approachable. Philosophy becomes *eteology*. "What is necessary today to turn the tide of our situation," Gebser writes, "are not new philosophemes, like the phenomenological, ontological, or existential, but eteologemes. Eteology must replace philosophy just as philosophy once replaced the myths."[20] When the mental is restored to its appropriate relation to the whole we are no longer in danger of making deficient and totalizing truth claims, (Sri Aurobindo's concept higher mind, as well as the supramental, are corroborative here).

The structures of consciousness and their mutational process as a whole, then, is the unfolding of time-space realizations (in the form of increasing dimensionality), an increasing remoteness from origin, and the gradual concrescence of individuation. Because

20 Gebser, *EPO*, 361.

the structures are always latent and present in us, and the future informs the present as much as the past, we cannot say this mutational process is linear. Taken as a whole, it is a series of punctuated leaps—restructurations—as worlds simultaneously close down and open up (Socrates bemoaned the loss of philosophy as an *oral* tradition as the Greeks moved into scribal culture). Discontinuity does not preclude integration, however: in the integral mutation is where we see a cohering of the whole.[21]

Gebser's conception of emergence without development and the synairetic crystallization of the structures is a profoundly novel departure from most literature on the subject of cultural evolution. Comparatively, Ken Wilber's insight on the Pre-Trans Fallacy, while helping us to avoid the same Traditionalist trappings by restoring transpersonal realities to higher stages of consciousness development, *still* retains a perspectival linearity that reduces the previous structures (the magic and mythic especially) to a state of mere

---

21 Although, from this aperspectival perception, the *entire* mutational process, and not just the integral leap, could be seen as an integral whole. The integral mutation is where this wholeness comes to the forefront, i.e., from maximum latency to full and conscious expression.

infantilism.[22] Here we are reminded of J.R.R. Tolkien's famous poem and manifesto, *Mythopoeia*, which
responds to something said by C.S. Lewis: that myths
were mere "lies breathed through silver." "There is no
firmament," writes Tolkien in reply, "only a void, unless a jeweled tent... myth-woven and elf-patterned;
and no earth, unless the mother's womb whence all
have birth."[23] Myths, myth-making, and, indeed, the
mythical structure of consciousness cannot be viewed
fixedly from the perspectival lens and still be appro-

22 See Ken Wilber, *The Collected Works of Ken Wilber, Volume 2* (Boston: Shambhala, 1999), 59. Wilber essentially claims there are two
camps when it comes to viewing pre-modernity. The first are the
Romantics, who see pre-modern people as living in a veritable
transpersonal paradise (a kind of unity consciousness). The other, more modernist viewpoint is to see any transpersonal state as
a regression (for example, Freud's famous claim that mysticism
was a mere return to the oceanic consciousness of the womb).
One claim is elevationist, while the other is reductive. This leaves
us with a tricky form of thinking, in that Wilber's developmental
solution necessitates a strictly linear view of consciousness emergence, saving the transpersonal for the higher stages while still
reducing the so-called "lower" stages to childlike fantasy rather
than a true and now lost mode of participation. The earlier stages are thus only validated insofar as they are prompted to grow
up and through into modernism, only later realizing spiritual dimensions at the level of the transpersonal. As it stands, this perspectival synthesis is incompatible with Gebser's thinking on the
structures. Where Wilber's thinking dovetails with Gebser's is in
his suggestion of dormancy, and unfolding, in the earlier stages.

23 See J.R.R. Tolkien, "Mythopoeia," in *Tree and Leaf, including the
Poem Mythopeia* (Boston: Houghton Mufflin, 1988), 99.

priately rehabilitated (indeed the perspectival lens is
something like a corrosive to enchanted and participatory life worlds). Fortunately, Gebser's suggestion that
the structures are all themselves a series of "discontinuous" transformations implicates their non-linearity
and frees them from a strictly developmental trajec-
tory.[24] This insight allows us to rightly place a certain
ontological validity in the earlier structures while also
acknowledging the gains of the later ones (the mythical, as we will see, in the emergence of the soul and the
mental in the emergence of the ego). At any rate, the
structures themselves continue to be effective (though
not always *efficient*), and not at all merely regressive
traits or evolutionary vestiges from an enchanted past.
The latter view reeks not only of the narrowing vision
of the mental-rational structure but also its colonizing
thought processes.[25] All mutations are phenomenologically co-present in human consciousness. "We are
convinced," Gebser writes, "of the continuous effectuality of the 'earlier' structures in us and the incipient,

24 Gebser, *EPO*, 42.

25 It is worth more than a footnote, but for this book we might place
a seed: the structures of consciousness are a mode of de-coloniza-
tion of animistic and participatory lifeworlds, indeed a decoloni-
zation of the soul in the last regard, even for the West. At the very
least the integral structure must be this, if it is anything

i.e., present effectuality of the so-called 'future structure.'"[26] Remember Rilke: "There is no place that does not see you."

Gebser's mutational approach, then, is *discontinuous*, offering us a careful way to talk about the future, about becoming, which of course involves some form of emergence through the processes of chronological time (i.e., humanity's progressive realization of origin).

This process is *not* developmental in a strict sense, since mutational leaps do not always necessitate a healthy integration of their previous structures (i.e., the "holonic" view of human evolution), even if they depend on a certain unfolding dimensionality.

We can steer clear of the twentieth century's debunked positivism while also avoiding our own era's deconstructionism, which, we will see, is arguably *still* a form of perspectival fixation through ratio.

The Archaic Structure
"Dreamlessly the true men of earlier times slept"

Here, *all* of the mutations of consciousness are present in a state of dormancy. Gebser makes note that *archaic*, in Greek, is *arche*, meaning "inception" or

26 Gebser, *EPO*, 43.

"origin."[27] This structure is *zero dimensional*, "a time where the soul is yet dormant, a time of complete non-differentiation of man and the universe."[28] Of all the structures, this is the most difficult to relate to any particular historical manifestation. Gebser's archaic, if we might point to it generally in cultural evolution, is the event horizon of hominization itself; that indecipherable gap between what makes us art-making human beings or pre-artistic hominid ancestors (yet, even *this* line is blurry and arguably some form of symbolic thinking could have been evidenced in earlier anthropoids). This attempt at a demarcation would have to be very roughly approximated, as the evolutionary process from *Australopithecus* to *Homo sapiens* has taken place over the past million years or so (where, exactly, would we pinpoint it?).

We find more evidence for the archaic's spiritual, rather than historical, expressions in the writings of Chuang-tzu: "Dreamlessly the true men of earlier times slept."[29] Feuerstein writes that the archaic, "denotes a consciousness of maximum latency and minimum

27 Ibid.
28 Ibid.
29 Ibid., 44.

transparency," which further helps us here.[30] We can recall the Greek myth of the Androgyne—the cellular-like unity of man and woman in a perfect sphere—but even this is still too laden with the mythical imagistic structure. Deep, dreamless sleep is a more direct expression of the archaic if we would attempt to encounter this structure in ourselves. Gebser uses a description by Richard Wilhelm (known for his well-read translation of *The I-Ching or the Book of Changes*), who notes that early Chinese chromatic symbolism had not yet differentiated blue and green, or earth and sky. "This identity of earth and sky is an expression of the macro-cosmic harmony... nothing less than *the perfect identity of* man *and universe.*"[31]

The emerging distinction of earth from sky, soul from world, was the first act of the soul's springing forth from dormancy (and hence out from the archaic's *total* identification with the world in deep slumber). Ken Wilber, in his earlier works such as *Up From Eden*, adapts Gebser's archaic structure as the archaic-ouroboric stage (Ouroboros being the serpent that devours itself, implicating non-differentiation). Gebser relates this discussion of earth and sky with Plato's statement

30 Feuerstein, *Structures of Consciousness*, 51.

31 Gebser, *EPO*, 44.

that, "the soul [came into being] simultaneously with the sky."[32]

There is not much that can be said, or documented, about the archaic, but the nature of this structure, as Feuerstein noted, is "maximum latency," meaning that all future mutations (magic, mythic, mental) are co-present and latent; the archaic is the latent integral, and the integral is the fully realized archaic. We can also say that the archaic's latency is inherently unstable; that the structures of consciousness are in some sense leaning onto their own potentiation, waking to spring forth.

And so we move to the first recognizable leap.

The Magic Structure

We leap from the zero dimensional identity of the archaic to the one dimensional pointed unity in the magical structure. This pointedness is two-fold for Gebser: it expresses the emerging differentiation of self from world while at the same denoting a world where every point is exchangeable with all other points in a vital, magical nexus. We have roused, ever slightly, from latent dreamlessness into deep, timeless dream-

32 Ibid.

ing, and in this dreaming there is a budding agency of the self-and-world distinction.

In magic, there is *making*. Reminding us again of the importance of etymology, Gebser links the words "magic," "make", "mechanism," "machine" and "might" with *mag(h)*.[33] Human beings in this structure begin to *have* a world rather than be identified *as* the world, and with the magical structure comes the activity of making and magic itself. William Irwin Thompson comments on the magic structure with a McLuhan-esque note:

> As *Homo sapiens sapiens* was emerging and branching off from archaic *Homo sapiens* in South Africa, the animal was the sloughed-off environment in the new invisible environment of humanity. Art emerged and became the difference that made a difference between nature and culture, and the first expressions of this division between the given and the gift were mobiliary objects, tools, musical instruments, and then parietal art and sculpture.[34]

33 Ibid, 46.
34 Thompson, *Beyond Religion*, 13.

The boundaries between self and world, culture and nature in this structure are more like a permeable cell wall than a city wall, however, and so the consciousness of the magical is marked by its capacity to *merge* with nature, to slip into trance, or what Imants Baruss describes in the plural as "alterations of consciousness."[35] Waking mind slips into dreaming mind—the two have yet to be cleaved into the recognizably modern sensibility. They operate in a different way, in a continuum: "The emerging personal ego is not yet stabilized and the labile mind can function in both the dreaming and waking consciousness at the same time. The individual sees the world, but the dreaming mind riffs on the precept and transforms it into two objects at once."[36] This *irruption of art into consciousness*, which we visited briefly in the previous chapter exploring the world-as-cave, poses serious questions. J.F. Martel in *Reclaiming Art* asks: "How can a life form evolved to survive and reproduce suddenly interrupt the automatic drift of reflex and instinct to produce *meaningful* images in pictures, songs, sculptures, poetry, and dance?"[37] This

---

35 See Imants Baruss, *Alterations of Consciousness: An Empirical Analysis for Social Scientists* (Washington DC: American Psychological Association, 2004).

36 Thompson, *Beyond Religion*, 14.

37 Martel, *Reclaiming Art in the Age of Artifice*, 8.

question is rhetorical, invoking the acausality of creativity itself. "Art was an event," Martel continues, "in the end art may not be our invention at all... Picasso got it wrong: the early humans didn't invent art. Art invented humanity."[38]

This insight seems to concur with Gebser's understanding that consciousness is not *ours*; we might speak of its realization *in* us but it is not, in truth, ours to possess. Rather, creativity and the structures of consciousness themselves are an *originary* phenomena (and therefore can only be traced back to the spiritual, the ineffable). Rather than heroically taking a leap into a new consciousness, each spiritual mutation is participatory process of entrusting oneself to origin and stepping into a process that is co-enactive rather than territorialized (merely taking, claiming, or conquering a time-space realization). Renaissance artists of the perspectival age were, after all, "*possessed* by, and did not merely *possess*, the urge to realize space."[39] To the degree we have any choice at all in this matter is our capacity to work *with* these forces that spring up through us; our capacity to allow and co-enact the coming of consciousness realization.

38 Ibid., 9.
39 Gebser, *EPO*, 41.

To summarize briefly, the magical structure's qualities manifest in their:

1) egolessness,

2) point-like unity

3) spaceless and timeless dimensionality

4) capacity to merge with nature and

5) humanity as *maker*

What Thompson describes as the ability of the magical structure to see both a material object and its symbolic counterpart is what William Blake poetically described as a "double vision,"

> *With my inward eye, 'tis an old Man gray*
> *With my outward a thistle across my way*[40]

For Gebser, this is the "visible interchangeability of the real and the symbolic," relaying the point-like unity of the magical structure, "in which each and every thing intertwines and is interchangeable."[41] Any one point is

---

40 William Blake as quoted in: Stephen Toulmin, "The Inwardness of Mental Life," *Critical Inquiry* 6.1 (1979): 1–16, 4.

41 Gebser, *EPO*, 48.

a secret passage all points. Yesterday, today, and tomorrow are interchangeable. Ritual acts are inseparable from their desired outcomes, and they are not causal as we would think (that X ritual produces Y result). Instead, for the magical structure, X *is* Y. Material reality *is* symbolic reality, full of the wonder and terror of other agencies and powers (in other words, the magical structure reveals the reality of animism). As moderns, we would think this means that the symbolic is *literalized* in the magical. This is not so. The magical is neither purely symbolic nor literal, the latter of which is a perspectival innovation and has no place being projected back into the magical structure. The magical world is a liminal substance, to which we must answer an ambiguous "yes" to the question of whether or not it is made up of matter or meaning.

Yet, even here, with humanity-as-maker, the beginnings of the *self* are nascent. "Although man fits in and merges with the event, this very merger and fusion give the event a definite direction... all directing implies a conscious process."[42] The act of producing art, magic, and making for the magical consciousness tells us that humanity is no longer in total identification with the world; the "gradual emergence of the ego" is setting in,

42 Ibid., 49.

even only as a group-ego, or group-consciousness.[43]

Shamanism is comfortable in this nexus state of liminality and trance. The Löwenmensch (the "Li-on-human") of the Upper Paleolithic (discovered in Germany),[44] "The Sorcerer" of Les Trois Frere, or the "Bird Man" of Lascaux are all powerful examples of human-animal, nature-culture, symbolic-material, and so on. Yet, another motif Gebser describes is that of *mouthlessness*. He uses the Wandjina rock art of the Australian Aborigines,[45] or the Venus of Brassempouy, to demonstrate:

> What this mouthlessness means is immediate-ly apparent when one realizes to what extent these paintings and statuettes are expression of the magic structure—but not yet of the mythi-cal structure. Only when myth appears does the mouth, to utter it, also appear... [It] indicates to what extent magic man placed significance on what he heard, that is, on the sounds of nature, and not on what was spoken.[46]

43 Ibid., 50.

44 See Jill Cook, "The Lion Man: An Ice Age Masterpiece,": https://blog.britishmuseum.org/the-lion-man-an-ice-age-masterpiece/ [last accessed 30 Dec 2018].

45 Gebser, *EPO*, 56.

46 Ibid, 57.

This capacity for silence, or *listening* marks the "labyrinthine ear," and not the eye, as the associative organ for the magical structure. Gebser again directs us to the word *gehören* ("to belong"), which derives from *hören* ("to hear").[47] Think back (*harken* back) again to the world-as-cave and the importance of acoustic space in the unperspectival enclosure to sympathetically resonate with voices in the dark. On another McLuhan-esque note, think of how the acoustics of the Greek amphitheater carried the magical structure into agrarian society. Memory, body posture, and lyricism played an important role for oral cultures before the predominance of written language.

I might add, however, that a *different* form of eye is important and shows up here in these mouthless visages—one which Gebser does not explicitly mention—and again links human beings *back* to the non-human surround of the animal world: picture the silent gaze of a deer in the forest, an owl's piercing vision—such wordless glances and visceral encounters communicate *volumes* in the non-verbal communication of body language and the subtle auditory environments common in the more-than-human world. The capacity for hearing is well developed in many species, not the least

47 Ibid, 60.

of which include our domesticated feline and canine companions.

The mouthless visage is a simultaneous harkening *back* to the embodied language of the animal world and the intuitive or *psychic* communication with the spirit world (these two worlds we should for the animistic magical structure form a *continuum* with the human world, as is so powerfully displayed in the aural visages of the Wandjina rock art).

Whenever we begin to reconnect with the non-verbal world of embodied presence and listening (in every sense of that word), when we begin to *hear* and so *gehören*—belong—to what we hear, we *attune* (there, hearing again) ourselves to the magical structure.

In its deficient phase, the magical structure has the capacity to overwhelm and undo ego consciousness, or else rigidify it into superstition (Gebser places "spell crafting" as the *efficient* and "witchcraft" as the *deficient* manifestations respectively, but we can rightly critique this choice of wording for its outdated and patriarchal bias towards witchcraft as a pejorative.)[48] We have already noted the etymological intimacy between make, machine, and magic in *mag*, but when the ego is over-inflated (and, hence, when the magic is repressed),

48 See, for example, Laura Tempest Zakroff's *The New Aradia: A*

it becomes ironically susceptible to a kind of possession by the powers and forces of the psychical world (the mythic and magical). These are often deficient, rather than efficient, retrievals. Gebser understood this as one of the underlying phenomena behind twentieth-century Europe's fascism (and so, unfortunately, in our own time). The magical is also deficiently expressed as the capacity to be mindlessly destructive a *doing without consciousness*,[49] which also manifests as a kind of machine consciousness, or mass destructive violence, in the deficient mental age.

We can leap forward—if only for a moment—to our own time where the structures of consciousness are *all* at play and look to the imagistic medium of cinema. In Stanley Kubrick's *The Shining*, Jack Torrence's waking ego is summarily dismantled and subsumed by the possessive and violent spirits of the Overlook Hotel; he succumbs to trancelike states, or becomes emotionally distraught by horrific waking dreams and violent nightmares (again, that collapse of distinction between the waking and dreaming mind). Note, even, the myth-

Witch's Handbook to Magical Resistance (Seattle: Revelore Press, 2018) or Pam Grossman's *Waking the Witch: Reflections on Women, Magic and Power* (New York: Gallery Books, 2019).

49 Gebser, *EPO*, 60.

ical temporality of Jack's murderous possession, which appears to mythically recur at the hotel, or the magical labyrinthine (or cave-like) quality of the Overlook Hotel itself (not to mention the film's labyrinth, which ultimately traps Jack like the Greek Minotaur).[50] It would seem that horror (especially supernatural horror) as an artistic genre in the contemporary world is a means for the magical structure—to the degree that its reality is rejected by the waking mental reality—to reassert itself with a vengeance.

Other, more efficient expressions of the magical come to mind in our contemporary media ecology. The artwork of the Peruvian shaman Pablo Amaringo, for instance, vividly demonstrates the magical structure's multitudinous interweaving. Stunning webs of colorful patterns reveal the complex unity of plant, human, animal, and spirit—this is visually concretized in the shaman's ceremonial *icaro* song performed during Ayahuasca ceremonies. This *singing back to the world*, often for the purposes of healing, is a powerful expression of the efficient and auditory magical.[51]

50 See John David Ebert, "John David Ebert Movie Review on *The Shining*":   https://www.youtube.com/watch?v=GJfzyxmWB3Y [last accessed 15 Oct 2018].

51   See Luis Eduardo Luna, Pablo Amaringo, *Ayahuasca Visions: The Religious Iconography of a Peruvian Shaman* (Berkeley: North

The revivified interest in shamanism, the retrieval of occult and esoteric practices, and Terence McKenna's "archaic revival" of the 1980s and 1990s also express a healthier form of re-integration of the magical structure in our time (and, for McLuhan, a resonance between electronic culture and oral culture, or the magic and mythic and the integral).[52]

For now, we can summarize the magical as the dimensional point: a navigation of thresholds in the shamanic liminality of the human and animal, a budding ego and group ego, a continuity of the waking world and spirit world, and a unity of the so-called "material" and symbolic realm.

This is the nexus of magical interweaving.

The ego exists as hardly anything but latency. The world nexus of being is yet to be *interiorized* and folded into the ego in the process of individuation. If a dimension of time manifests here, then it is a *timelessness*: the unity of past, present, and future. One part for all parts. *Pars pro toto.*

Atlantic Books, 1999).

52 See Terrence McKenna, *The Archaic Revival* (San Francisco: Harper Collins, 1991).

The Mythical Structure

As we move from the one-dimensional magical structure to the two-dimensional mythical structure, we unfold into the quality of *polarity*. Timelessness leaps into rhythmicity. The mythical structure expresses itself in the circularity of winter and summer, the astronomical cycles of cosmogony, the complementarity of heaven and the underworld, and the mirroring of the microcosm and macrocosm in the individual soul and the world soul (the *Anima Mundi*). The self in the mythical cosmos remains participatory, but its diffusiveness gives way to a centering in the soul through a process of the interiorization.

It is difficult to make any sharp distinctions between the magical and mythical structures (to make the cut, or ratio, as it were). Arguably these two structures intermingle as far back as the irruption of art-making itself. For in the interweaving of the vital web of the magical we also have the interlinking of earth and sky, stars and spirits, star time and seasonal time. Indeed the stars the source of some of our earliest and most archetypal narratives as described in Gordon White's *Star.Ships*. The magical interweaving nexus continues to appear in the mythic structure as a motif. Gebser gives us the example of ancient Egyptian drawing of a "Nubian Battle" on a chest in Tutankhamen's tomb, circa 13,000 BCE: soldiers appear in battle, depicting as an interlinked, unperspectival mesh.[53] The shamanic morphology of human-into-animal also continues to show up in Meso-American civilizations through examples like the Olmec's "jaguar man."[54]

"The essential characteristic of the mythical structure," Gebser writes, "is the emergent awareness of soul."[55] Souls and stars, astronomical time and archetypal time are therefore synonymous with the consciousness of the mythical structure. Gobekli Tepe, which dates back to the Upper Paleolithic (further entangling the magic and mythic structures), or even the Neolithic Stonehenge, express this complex, astrological awareness. It also manifests in the sophisticated calendrical systems of the Maya, the Aztec and Egyptian civilizations (indeed the entirety of the ancient world was acutely aware of the stars). Interestingly, Gebser understands this cosmological orientation as a final move out from the magical structure's nexus—a fully realized leap as nature becomes mastered through cosmology and the ancient sciences.

53 Gebser, *EPO*, 53.
54 Thompson, *Beyond Religion*, 14.
55 Gebser, *EPO*, 61.

When we speak of myth and soul, however, we must speak of *image*, and perhaps nothing express-es this mutational leap from magic to mythic better than the multidimensional image of the "Prince with a Crown of Feathers," an ancient wall fresco from Knos-sos, Crete. As Gebser details, this image:

> ...expresses man's extrication from his intertwin-ing with nature in two ways: first, by presenting terrestrial man (and not a divinity) standing out in partial relief from the background which sur-rounds and protects him, and thereby depict-ing the body in partial extrication from his sur-roundings; and second, by placing the upper torso against the "sky"—"the sky is simultaneous with the soul," and, we would add, is also "simultane-ous with time."[56]

The Prince is no longer defined or enmeshed in the veg-etative nexus of nature but is now kin to his own soul and the stars that correspond with him. Surrounding him are blooming lilies, but "the lilies," Gebser writes, "is a nature already illuminated. The body itself, with its almost flower-like form and natural grace, crowned

56 Ibid., 63.

by a head which looks above and over the earth."[57] The Prince's head is adorned by feathers, not flowers or vines, and birds are a symbol for soul. And so here we have a complex image of the soul emerging into consciousness and taking its celestial station.

We move away from the magical visage of the mouthless face, which points us back to the liminality of the magical. The mouth must now speak, but even the word myth expresses this structure's polarity. The word *myth* has its etymological ties to *mouth* and "speech, word," or "report." The corresponding verb, "mu," means "to sound." Yet another verb with the same root, *myein*, means "to close the mouth," eyes, and wounds, and the Latin *mutus* meaning "to be silent."[58] So we have the mythic polarity of speech and silence; the uttering of myth and the contemplation of the mysteries in fecund silence. *The visible and invisible.*

This duality is the mythic structure's two-dimensionality (read: unperspectival), a diurnal world consisting of night and day, waking and dreaming, Hades and Olympus, Yin and Yang, or the Andean indigenous concept Yanintin and Masintin.[59] These poles make up

57 Ibid.

58 Ibid., 64.

59 See Hillary S. Webb, *Yanantin and Masintin in the Andean World:*

complementary, but not yet contradictory opposites. Contradiction would emerge later, in the mental structure, where the irreconcilability of opposites would break the cyclic round in favor of a consciousness of innovation, and therefore a new time form.

The soul emerges as *persona* (which, mind you, literally means "mask"), the Other, whom we meet in the dramaturgical movement of the stars. It is through the persona, through the mask, that any future ego consciousness can ever emerge ("per-sona" means "to sound through"). Before the individuated appearance of modern ego, the "I" reveals itself as if through a dark mirror (think of Narcissus staring into his pool). Here is the archetypal drama of the soul, psyche: not as singular "I" but a plurality of constellated archetypes and cyclical progressions (think again of the starry night sky, charged with cosmological significance and to which the individual makes up the complementary pole, a mirror of the microcosm and microcosm). The inward-facing mythical structure is a coming to consciousness of the person-as-soul, and in the mysteries, like Eleusis, the silence makes up another polarity as the complementarity of utterance and occlusion;

Complementary Dualism in Modern Peru (Albuquerque: University of New Mexico Press, 2009).

hidden and revealed; the uninitiated and the initiate.

The mythical structure alternates between timelessness and time, the eternal return and rhythmic periodicity, mundane and sacred time.[60] Seeded in this consciousness of time, however, is the coming of the mental world.

"Very nearly all myths contain an element of consciousness emergence."[61] Thompson reminds us, par excellence, how myth, when read in a non-literal way, helps to render the invisible processes of cultural evolution visible. We can see many myths of the ancient world beginning to express this move from the mythical structure to the mental structure through the motif of the sea voyage, which reflects humanity's precarious relationship to the deep waters of psyche.

The sea is often utilized as an image of the soul, upon which daring heroes (nearly all *men* in these myths) go on to battle gods and monsters—*The Odyssey* being one such myth. These men embark on adventures of self-making by pitting themselves against cosmic forces and dangerous powers of the soul. It is Odysseus himself who utters the prototypical announcement of ego: *"Eim Odysseus"* ("am Odysseus"),

60 Gebser, *EPO*, 67.
61 Ibid, 69.

although Gebser mentions how the lack of "I" in this statement marks only a budding mental ego.[62] Even Narcissus, in his myth, is looking into the water—his soul—and in doing so is becoming self-consciously aware of his existence.[63]

This leads us to another prototypical element of the nascent mental structure: *wrath*. "Wrath or anger is the force which bursts the confines of community and clan, to the extent that it manifests the 'hero' in the individual and spurs him on toward further individuation, self assertion, and consequently ego-emergence," Gebser writes. The word, mental, itself relates to the Greek *menis*, which literally means "wrath," "courage," and the Latin *mens*, denoting "intent, anger, thought, deliberation," and so on.[64]Lord Krishna commands Arjuna to go forth and do his duty on the battlefield. The *Iliad* begins with the line, "Sing, goddess, the *wrath* of Peleus' son Achilles."[65] The Biblical God of the Old Testament also manifests this quality as divine wrath. We can move back further, as Thompson does, and recognize this same ego consciousness emerging in the wrathful

62 Ibid., 71.
63 Ibid., 70.
64 Ibid., 75.
65 Ibid, 71.

heroism of Gilgamesh and Enkidu, who, recognizing and fearing their own mortality, set out to battle the old nature gods of the magical structure and wrest from a wise sage the secrets of eternal life. Like a good mythic-to-mental narrative, however, the theme is not one of ultimate triumph but tragedy and the existential contemplation of mortality: the king is only able to achieve alienation and death.[66] Enkidu dies of a cursed illness and Gilgamesh returns to his kingdom defeated.

This existentialism expresses another duality of the mythic: the ego is both delighted in their self-becoming and agonized by the awareness of their tragic impermanence (and ultimately, impotence). The goddess Athena bursts forth—fully armored!—from the head of Zeus. "Every 'novel' thought will tear open wounds,"[67] Gebser writes. Athena is owl-eyed, she sees through the night as if it were day, and her city, Athens, becomes the locus of the new *logos*: the philosopher's Academy.

66 William Irwin Thompson, *Coming Into Being: Artifacts and Texts in the Evolution of Consciousness* (New York: St. Martin's Griffin, 1998), 155.

67 Gebser, *EPO*, 75.

The Mental Structure

The mental structure announces the coming of the ego, and as we have hopefully provided thorough examples in the previous chapter (Ch. 4, "Three Worlds"), the perspectival world is the mental world of spatialized consciousness. The mental breaks out of rhythmic time and moves us into linear time, into progression and the very concept of historical time. Here we also conceive of a clock-like cosmos of rational order (the dialectic), and the churning of mechanical gears (motoricity) to denote the spatialization of time. If the magic is *the point*, and the mythic is the polarized *circle*, then the mental is *the triangle*. Recall the triadic cone of perspectival space, the point-of-view, which is itself composed of three points: two from the observer and traced into the one—the vanishing point—of the event horizon. The mental triangle is a momentous rupture from the mythic membrane. Gebser illustrates:

> This process is an extraordinary event which is literally earth-shaking; it bursts man's protective psychic circle and congruity with the psychic-naturalistic-cosmic-temporal world of polarity and enclosure. The ring is broken, and man steps out of the two-dimensional surface into space, which

he will attempt to master by his thinking. This is an unprecedented event, an event that fundamentally alters the world.[68]

In the mythical structure there is what Gebser describes as *oceanic thinking* which circles around the numinous content of the world. For instance, Heraclitus writes in this fragment: "for souls it is death to become water; for water it is death to become earth. But from the earth comes water and from water, soul."[69] Circumscribing around something, in this case, death, "is a vivid demonstration that the mythical circular world has a content," but in the emerging mental, which ruptures the circle with directional thinking, "mental man... lost his content; for space is without content."[70] This new content-less spatial plane is at first still potent with creative exuberance and fervor; the mental subject is now an individual, and so goes forth in a frenzy of creative mutations in perspectival art and the new spatializing, quantifying science (consider the expansion of empiricism, map-making, and new mathematical innovations between the thirteenth and fifteenth

68 Ibid.
69 Ibid., 252
70 Ibid., 253.

centuries), but, when it enters its deficient mode, ratio, the spatial plane becomes increasingly content-less, eroding the qualitative dimensions of the cosmos in favor of a purely measurable and void matter (the feminine "mother" is exchanged for the de-souled and re-tooled mental "matter"). The subjective and interior domains—consciousness itself—are left to be finally measured as mere epiphenomena in a materialism that has at last undone even the "man" who was once the measurer of all things. Ratio, in the last word, makes the cut upon itself.

Long before the deficient mental,[71] however, the emergence of the efficient mental structure was a novel mutation, expressed through examples like Plato's *diaresis*, a form of "conceptual hair-splitting" or "taking apart" style of thinking. "The polar constellation," or the mythic polarity, Gebser writes, "is no longer valid; what is valid are the parts which can be made into opposites."[72] In other words, discursive thought is born:

---

71 Ibid., 255. We can make the important discernment between the efficient and deficient mental with this statement: "Mental thought is still estimation (*ermessen*), while rational thinking is arrogant, calculation and presumption (*Anmassung*) which ultimately lead to the destructive fragmentation of human nature itself."

72 Ibid., 256.

...In the imagery of the polar, mythical, and symbolic expression, both were possible: the "not-on-
ly-but-also" was valid until Aristotle's premise of
tertium non datur annulled its force for two mil-
lennia in favor of the unambiguous "either-or.[73]

Mythical opposites have become inherently unstable in the emerging mental structure. Ambiguity becomes impossible—it must be resolved by a tertiary
element (or else the resolution must be either-or). In
contrast to *oceanic thinking* in the mythical we have
pyramidal thinking in the mental. Here we can further
describe Hegel's famous dialectic of thesis, antithesis, and synthesis as the prototypical formulation of
mental thought: a thesis instigates its opposite, the
antithesis, and through the inherent tension of their
opposition produces a new synthesis.[74] The machinery
of history—or the history of ideas—rotates for Hegel
and many modernist thinkers according to this triadic
gyration of progress.

We find further examples of triadic thinking
through the rise of monotheism in the Christian trinity

73 Ibid, 257.

74 Even the language of "objectivity" implies this oppositional quality: an object is a noun, an item to be measured in space, but it is
also a verb, the action, *to object* to something.

of Father, Son, and Holy Spirit, or the Abrahamic triad
of humanity, prophet (as mediator), and God, or even
the Neoplatonic conceptions of a mediating realm, the
World Soul, between the realm of matter and the One
(Zoroastrianism and later, Christianity, also develop an
oppositional cosmology between a Heaven and a Hell
that must ultimately be vanquished). The directedness
of the emerging mental structure is, for the Abrahamic
traditions, an eschatological or future-oriented form
of time; *a movement from left to right.* "Know Thyself,"
inscribed over the temple in Delphi and protected by
the wakeful god, Apollo, is written from left to right,[75]
anticipating the very conceptualization of "clockwise" and "counter clockwise." The word *direct* itself
betrays its bias (*richten*). "Since ancient times, the left
side has stood for the side of the unconscious or the
unknown," Gebser writes, "the right side, by contrast,
has represented the side of consciousness and wakefulness."[76] Directing, judging, and law (in German, justice
is *Rechtsprechung*) requires a wakeful mind—it "sets
things straight"—and so it is no surprise then that the
mental structure ushers in the age of paternal judg-
ment in the form of monotheism and the genealogical

75 Gebser, *EPO*, 78.

76 Ibid., 79.

line of male prophets and kings; laws and land. "Moses and Lycurgus open the age of patriarchy,"[77] but we should also remember McLuhan's alphabetic culture in Greece, which divides up spoken language into script. It was through writing that further leaps into the mental structure's characteristic abstraction were made possible. We move from the *image* to the *word*, from the mythos to the logos; it is the clarification of thinking, that is, wakeful conceptualization, that supplants the dreamlike mythical structure's psychical and imagistic consciousness.[78] Pythagoras dictated to his followers that one should enter the temple sanctuary from the right, even going so far as to suggest they remove their right shoe first.[79] Plato had allegedly written over his door: "No one unversed in geometry shall enter," that is, no one who cannot measure.[80] This is the move from the unperspectival world-as-cave, the dreaming world, to the wakeful solar world.

When Odysseus utters his famous words—"am Odysseus"—he does so only after washing up and

---

77 Ibid.

78 An interesting study of this move from image to word is found in Leonard Shlain's *The Alphabet Versus the Goddess* (New York: Penguin/Compass, 1998).

79 Gebser, *EPO*, 83.

80 Ibid., 84.

awakening to himself "on the rescuing shore," as if "spit out" from the mythical sea.[81] A few centuries later, the New Testament's miraculous tale of Jesus walking on water dynamically expresses a new mental consciousness no longer threatened by re-immersion into the imagistic and watery depths of soul.

The organ of the mental structure is the *eye*—that which measures and perceives. Its characteristic consciousness is not the sidereal realms of dream or the unconscious (psyche), nor is it the hollowed-out persona—that which is sounded through with the voice of the muses—but the buttressed and insulated fortress of the modern ego. The previous reality of permeability and magical sympathy with the spirit world, or the mythical eternal recurrence with the soul and World Soul, gradually recede behind us (behind the sectored "point of view"). Secularity in the West takes hold, and the reality of the magical nexus and mythical temporality evaporates like a dream soon after rousing to wakeful consciousness. Stirring from the waters of myth and on the newfound shoreline of perspectival space, the new mental subject moves from dreaming myth into waking history. The individual has come to the forefront, the one who has their rights and goes

81   Ibid., 91.

forth to conquer space. Religion leaves *religere* (to observe the mysteries) and necessarily becomes *religare* (to *tie-back* to the vanishing potency and powers of the previous structures).

For Parminedes, "thinking and being is one and the same," or Thomas Hobbes, "thinking is calculation in words," or Rene Descartes, "I think, therefore I am," or even his contemporary the mathematician Pierre Gassendi's reply: "I walk about, therefore I am," such statements represent for Gebser the mental's active orientation: the ego "whose consciousness rests primarily in action and deed."[82] Mental activity is spatial activity, whether we are walking (such as Thoreau's classic 1851 treatise, for instance, called *Walking*), talking, or thinking our way through spatial reality. Indeed, how many philosophers and thinkers must go on their long sojourns through parks or cosmopolitan spaces to come to their realizations (this author included)! Gebser demonstrates the sheer spatiality of mental thought even as it retains its characteristic abstractness:

> Perspectival thinking spatializes and then employs what it has spatialized. All inferences or deductions are expressed in language by spatial

82 Ibid., 97.

concepts. Language speaks of "transcending"
or "overriding" or "exceeding," and philosophic
thought of this kind "represents, conceives of"
(*vorstellen*, literally "places before"); it "proves"
(*nachweisen*, literally "points to"); it "grasps" and
comprehends"; it "grasps conceptually" (*auffas-
sen*, literally "aches"); it "considers" (*überlegen*,
literally "turns over"); it "imputes" (*unterstellen*,
literally "places under"); it "debates" and "argues"
(*auseinandersetzen*, literally "takes apart").[83]

In its most brilliant and efficient expression, the mental is what contemporary philosopher Adam Robbert,
developing the concept from Pierre Hadot's *Philosophy as a Way of Life: Spiritual Exercises from Socrates to
Foucault*, rightly points out is a form of *askesis* (spiritual exercise), "we call this practice an askesis of the
'I'—of the self developing a relation to itself."[84] Here
is the efficient call of the mental to *know thyself*. The
mental, like all mutations, originates as a spiritual and
creative leap substantiated by origin itself. And so, to
know thyself is synonymous not only by a mental and
spatial knowing but a rendering transparent of that

83 Ibid., 258.
84 See Adam Robbert's personal blog, www.knowledge-ecology.
com, and *The Side View* project.

spatial knowledge and individuation to its spiritual
and diaphanous home. This spiritual quality is echoed
in Renaissance art and humanism, as we have already
briefly touched on in this volume, but it is worth invoking Giovanni Pico della Mirandola's *Oration on the
Dignity of Man.* In this fabled biblical conversation, God
speaks to Adam:

> But you, constrained by no limits, may determine
> your nature for yourself, according to your own
> free will... We have made you neither of heaven
> nor of earth, neither mortal nor immortal, that you
> may, as the free and extraordinary shaper of your-
> self, fashion yourself in whatever form you prefer.[85]

This notion of self-fashioning in Pico's humanist text
becomes the spiritual call of Western philosophy, art,
and culture, and echoes centuries after the Renaissance in the individuating quality of the literary novel.
The mental affords us the possibility to self-fashion,
and as Gebser points out, this is a tremendous responsibility to bear; one that the hypertrophied ego is not
sufficient to live up to the task in fulfilling. But the

85 Giovanni Pico della Mirandola, *Oration on the Dignity of Man*, ed.
and trans. Francesco Borghesi, Michael Papio, and Massimo Riva
(Cambridge: Cambridge UP, 2012), 117.

promise of the mental (if it can be said that there is one) is that it indeed points to a future realized *co-creative* capacity: to become co-fashioners of our cosmos. This participatory turn is what Richard Tarnas, in *The Passion of the Western Mind*, sees as our ultimate task for tomorrow,[86] and what Sri Aurobindo understood to be part of the ontological pull of our supramental and divinized future. "In creativity, origin is present," Gebser writes, "and creativity is something that 'happens' to us, that fully effects or fulfills itself in us."[87] The efficient mental structure is perhaps a harbinger for tomorrow's integral human mutation; a human species that has effectually become not the self-serving ego of a narrowed materialism but a diaphanous spiritual being in a participatory relationship with origin's creative and mutational process. Since all structures are present in us, we can individually decide to orient ourselves towards such a future, as Gebser gently and repeatedly instructs throughout his body of work this is not only a mental *action* but an integral *allowing*, and as Aurobindo also indicates through the individuated practice of integral yoga.

---

86   See Richard Tarnas, *The Passion of the Western Mind* (New York: Random House, 1991).

87   Gebser, *EPO*, 313.

The Mental Crisis, or
Prelude to the Integral Structure

> "Mutational periods are times of
> disturbance and even destruction."
> —Jean Gebser[88]

As we conclude this chapter we can hopefully appreciate the wondrous potency of each of the mutations as they have unfolded in their dimensionality: the deep, dreamless, and latent sleep of the archaic, the dreaming timelessness of the magical nexus, the imagistic power and starry rhythmicity of the soul in the mythic, and the wakeful, spatial exuberance and glorious self-discovery of the mental. Each structure manifests a unique expression of time and space (even if that means it is timeless or spaceless), self and self-consciousness. Each structure expresses its own world, its own ontological reality, which we can now hopefully appreciate without assuming the wakeful, mental claim to exclusive objectivity. If the mental cannot "measure" the measureless, it is not real, but we know that this attitude is the equivalent of an amnesiac who has been cut off from the presence of their living past.

88 Ibid., 295.

The archaic, magical, and mythical worlds live on in us, if only as latent presences and, as we mentioned at the outset, sometimes *ghosts*. As we need to see in the following chapter—and as we mentioned in the initial description of the perspectival world—the mental in its later disenchanted and deficient rational phase becomes increasingly undone by the dimension of time itself.

The eye of the spatial world is rendered, at last, too narrow a perspective, and the ego too rigid a self-sense, for the "open expanse of the open world."[89] The objects of the aperspectival world are no longer opaque, they open up into a new transparency: "What is gaining importance now is the spiritual light reigning between objects—the tension and the relation between them," Gebser writes in *Rilke and Spain* concerning the new aperspectival forms of expression in poetry.[90]

Space becomes transparent, and time becomes not a *quantitatively* measured clock but an ever-increasing *qualitative* intensity. The presence of the past looms large, the future seems to have its own gravitational pull, and the static spatial world begins to move.

---

89 Feuerstein, *Structures of Consciousness*, 170. Feuerstein's translated excerpt of Jean Gebser's *Decline and Participation*.

90 Feuerstein, *Structures of Consciousness*, 128. Feuerstein's translation.

Following the zenith of the mental structure's mastery of space, time becomes the central question and concern. But, unmastered, or un-realized by the incipient integral structure, time threatens to destroy the mental world just as Copernicus shattered the geocentrism of the unperspectival world:

> We are confronted here with the irruption of the fourth dimension into the three-dimensional world which in its first outburst shatters this three dimensional world. At first the unmastered time threatens to destroy space and its framework.[91]

Time begins to burst forth everywhere and initiates a crisis. With the advent of evolutionary theory, the very stones become temporally transparent, revealing to us the remnants of ancient life. *We* become transparent to our hominid ancestors (to the great dismay of the state of Tennessee) and in the crisis of climate change the future becomes transparent to us (unfortunately, our collective actions have become all too present for our descendants, too). Alfred Wegener's theory of continental drift reveals the geography of a static, spatial world to be in constant flux. Astronomy reveals a nearly

91 Gebser, *EPO*, 287.

unfathomable vastness (and emptiness) of space and deep cosmic time, while physics destroys the fluidic ether and renders space itself into time through Einstein's relativity.

Saving a full definition of time for the next chapter, we can say for now that time becomes a force pressing upon us; a new reality breaking through, but one for which the mental power of measurement is an insufficient response. Time irrupts as *a runaway force* in the uncontrollable march of technological upheaval and social revolution. It also manifests as a collective anxiety and unstoppable momentum: from the Atom Bomb to the Anthropocene.

In the next chapter we will explore what time *is* from the integral mutation, because what is increasingly needed as we move into the future is a consciousness of time: a new integral ontology that can respond to the multi-armed crisis currently facing our world. Only an integral consciousness has the capacity to concretize time and so translate what appears to be an uncontrollable force—time unmastered by the mental—to the conscious realization of time-free origin. The integral culture of the future is one that is no longer impotent to the forces that the mental world has unleashed but left unfinished. As Gebser says, the mental, "can merely initiate a world-transforming consciousness structure."[92] The forces that the mental world unleashes are the same forces that the integral consciousness realizes.

The late period of the mental structure is all too familiar to us. Following the Renaissance and the bursting forth of space we see the increasing rigidification and homogenization of complex cultures into static nationalities. "Nationalism is prototypical of three-dimensional thinking," Gebser writes, "to consider man as an offspring of a nation is to perceive the nature and ways of one's own nation as being an enduring ideal. Such a static view is a three-dimensional, perspectival, and fixed conception."[93] The homogenizing forces of McLuhan's print age helped to intensify this trend, and with colonialism and empire, we see the glory of the mental become soiled through the mass genocide of worldwide indigenous populations (not to mention the "fallout" of fossil fuels and ecological crisis that we currently face). The seemingly unstoppable eruption of violent revolution, world wars, and mass movements in the twentieth century were personal for Gebser, who was nearly killed trying to escape the border of Franco's Spain. He would change his name from the German "Hans" to the French "Jean" in 1931 and, like C. G. Jung,

92   Ibid., 284.
93   Ibid., 294.

ultimately settled in Switzerland for the remainder of his life.[94]

As alluded to earlier, the hypertrophied ego of the late mental consciousness is ironically susceptible to being overpowered by a regression to the deficient magical structure and its negative mass influence:

> Here we can discern the tragic aspect of the defi-
> cient mental structure…. Reason, reversing itself
> metabolistically to an exaggerated rationalism,
> becomes a kind of inferior plaything of the psy-
> che, neither noticing or even suspecting the con-
> nection… This negative link to the psyche, usurp-
> ing the place of genuine mental relation, destroys
> the very thing achieved by the authentic relation:
> the ability to gain insight into the psyche.[95]

In our own time, this same problem is evident in the perspectival and sectored fragments of online communities on Facebook and elsewhere: all falling prey to external influences (political, economic, or otherwise). The hyper-mediated egos of today insulate themselves within their own sectored reality, using the perspectiv-

---

94 Feuerstein, *Structures of Consciousness*, 25.
95 Gebser, *EPO*, 97.

al tool of "tunnel vision" to upend "facts" and inhabit their own "post-truth" world. The flood of mental knowledge has seemingly created its own opposite: as the internet is a "Janus-faced" manifestation, expressing both the promise of an aperspectival reality and the deficiencies of mental ratio, it is no surprise that it seems to both empower the failings of yesterday and the potentialities of tomorrow. James Bridle's recent *New Dark Age: Technology and the End of the Future* illustrates the failure of the technologically driven mental-rational consciousness to realize its techno-utopia; when sheer data overwhelms, we have only the splintering off of infinite sectored, perspectival realities, inducing a collapse of knowledge rather than a new, enlightened Information Age.[96]

We seem to face a fork in the road between planetization—the Teilhardian notion of an integral world civilization—and a new Dark Age, which William Irwin Thompson points out does tend to occur in "chaotic bifurcations" between major leaps of consciousness.[97] Yet, the aperspectival world must take hold if we are to have a future. The so-called "end of the future"

---

96 See James Bridle, *New Dark Age: Technology and the End of the Future* (Brooklyn: Verso, 2018).

97 See Thompson, *Coming Into Being.*

described by Bridle is really only the end of the mental world, and the "post-truth" world is expressing—as a *via negativa* manifestation—the end of the perspectival solidity. Tomorrow's integral world is one where a new solidity must be found, something perhaps akin to anthropologist Bruno Latour's aperspectival science where, rather than data, the whole ecology of human culture, knowledge construction, and the more than human world all come into play.[98]

Eco-philosopher Tim Morton's recent *Being Ecological* argues from this same, aperspectival orientation: that perspectival facts and "information dumps" are not enough. We must find another way to relate to people, or more accurately: to reveal to them how they are already ecological beings living in a symbiotic and (my choice word) aperspectival reality.[99] This emphasis on a new mode of perceiving the self-and-world has a mutational flavor and bears the integral marker of seeing through.

98 See, "Bruno Latour, the Post-Truth Philosopher, Mounts a Defense of Science," *New York Times*: https://www.nytimes.com/2018/10/25/magazine/bruno-latour-post-truth-philosopher-science.html [last accessed 1 Dec 2018].

99 See Timothy Morton, *Being Ecological* (Cambridge, MA: MIT Press, 2018). This book is arguably an excellent introduction to what aperspectival thinking looks like in the twenty-first century, the century of climate change.

Gebser's time is eerily prescient of our own. As we face the worldwide resurgence of fascism, "universal intolerance," and the collapse of perspectival solidity (and the meltdown of the perspectival nation-state), his words ring as uncomfortably true for us as they were for him and are worth quoting at length:

> As it [the perspectival world] developed over the centuries, this state of affairs gives rise to the most destructive of the stigmas of our age: the universal intolerance that prevails today, the fanaticism to which it leads. A person who is anxious, or who is fleeing from something, or who is lost either with respect to his own ego or with respect to the world—it holds equally true in both instances—is a person who will always be intolerant, as he feels threatened in his vital interest. He "sees" only a vanishing point lost in the misty distance (the vanishing point of linear perspective of which Leonardo once wrote); and he feels obliged to defend his point fanatically, lest he lose his world entirely.[100]

Perhaps it is only when the world is darkest that we might seek new pathways—new "lines of flight," as

100 Gebser, *EPO*, 23; brackets added by author.

Deleuze puts it—to at last try out for ourselves. So, it is my hope that the integral mutation can begin to shine a spiritual light on the narrowed, perspectival world, which is most assuredly now coming to some form of conclusion. Tomorrow, which we are about to discuss, is already present and we can find its characteristic qualities emerging everywhere in culture.

We have demonstrated the collapse of the mental world, but what of the new reality?

Seeing From All Sides

It is hopefully clearer now as to why the mental assessment of gradations, stages, levels, and other forms of spatialized thinking (such as the pyramidal dialectic) are not sufficient expressions of integrality. The mutations, being discontinuous leaps, demonstrate *both* a processual unfoldment—a coming-to-consciousness—and a non-linear co-presence and interdependence; the spiritual light reigning between objects is also reigning between the structures.[101]

For instance: is the imagistic psyche of the mythic

---

101 See Thompson, *Coming Into Being*, 14. Thompson put it nicely when he wrote: "Gebser's five structural mutations of consciousness should not be read as static stages or levels in a linear progression; they are processual transformations."

structure developmentally and categorically inferior or "lesser" to the mental structure's waking, discursive ego? The latter may unfold from the former, but their relationship is more akin to an organism's morphology: the petal to its stem, or the branches to the roots. Or even the qualitative "morphology" of consciousness states themselves: between waking, dreaming, and deep dreamless sleep, these states make up the dynamic wholeness of every human being.

We are what is visible and invisible, what is waking and what is occluded.

This new style of non-linear thinking places us upon a challenging precipice of thought: how might we express emergence *without* adhering to developmental thinking (this is not to completely denigrate the mental's spatial emphasis, but to dislodge our own perspectival fixity)? One approach would be, as Gebser suggests, to merely loosen it a bit, displaying some degree of aperspectival freedom; simply becoming aware of our tendency to spatialize reality as we study the structures of consciousness can help this process of "mental dislodgment," for lack of a better phrase.

The unfolding of consciousness and its increasing dimensionality are, "accompanied by an increasing reification or materialization of the world," but this is less a matter of gain or loss than a "remarkable kind of rearrangement."[102] It is in these turns of phrase that we really begin to see that Gebser's approach emphasizes discontinuity and non-linear emergence, while deemphasizing linearity and a developmental view (the unfoldment of dimensionality is acknowledged but not overextended into greater significance). At the very least—in Gebser's concept of *systasis*—we are pointed to something more than perspectival linearity: in this new definition of emergence, a "seeing from all sides," the past, present, and future dynamically inform a coherent whole and its manifold realizations.

This "seeing from all sides" notion anticipated the "postwar turn" in Western intellectual culture (exhibited by many French intellectuals as deconstruction, or later post-structuralism). It would be in 1980 that Deleuze and Guattari wrote about the aperspectival concept of a multiplicitous *rhizome* in *A Thousand Plateaus*. For Deleuze and Guattari, rhizomatic thinking is dynamic just like the plant root itself: the rhizome permits one to enter and move thought from any side (or, we could say now: from all sides) without regard for hierarchical or chronological procession. The latter form of thinking they described as *arborescent thinking*, which is characteristically linear and chronological

102   Gebser, *EPO*, 117, 119.

(i.e., mental and perspectival).[103] This idea also helps us begin to see the question surrounding us everywhere today of a networked society: in the "multitude" of Hardt and Negri,[104] the distributive "post-capitalist" initiatives of our time such as platform cooperatives, the experimental digital "cryptocurrencies," or in the work of media theorist Douglas Rushkoff to call out and rewrite the "source code" of unsustainable economic systems.[105] Last but certainly not least, it manifests in the call for an "ecology of mind" as anthropologist Gregory Bateson had described it and as Nora Bateson calls "symmathesy."[106]

The aperspectival turn is well underway, with no obvious or even necessary divide between the technological and ecological realms (indeed, these technologies of light are contingent upon their ecological resources and tied intimately with the mineralogical realm).

103 See Gilles Deleuze and Félix Guattari, *A Thousand Plateaus: Capitalism and Schizophrenia* (New York: Continuum, 2003).

104 See Michael Hardt, Antonio Negri, *Multitude: War and Democracy in the Age of Empire* (New York: Penguin, 2004).

105 See Douglas Rushkoff, *Throwing Rocks at the Google Bus* (New York: Portfolio/Penguin, 2017).

106 See Nora Bateson, *Small Arcs of Larger Circles: Framing Through Other Patterns* (Axminster: Triarchy Press, 2016).

The very crisis of climate change is a temporal question: of unforeseen consequences, in seeing the world as segmented divide rather than a whole in which we are constituted at the biospheric level.

Late capitalism—the ultimate extension of ratio— manifests the reductive quantification of *all* things into the mere measurable. To be Rushkoff's "team human," as he describes it, is to be an integral human being: to be *for* the whole and so for the future.[107] As the late Ursula K. Le Guin has popularized in recent years: "We live in capitalism. Its power seems inescapable. So did the divine right of kings... Resistance and change often begin in art."[108] These expressions point to a mutational potency in our present age: a willingness to take those originary and creative leaps into freedom.

An entirely new reality is opening up to us, and so we should begin an exploration of the integral structure.

107 See Douglas Rushkoff's podcast series, *Team Human*: https://teamhuman.fm/

108 See, Calla Wahlquist, "A Life in Quotes: Ursula K. Le Guin," *The Guardian*: https://www.theguardian.com/books/2018/jan/24/a-life-in-quotes-ursula-k-le-guin [last accessed 30 Nov 2018].

The Integral Mutation, or Diaphaneity

The integral leap implies an integration of *all* structures, a waring. This integration does not belong to the mental structure's capacity for wakeful synthesis, generalization, or categorization. "A mere conscious illumination of these states, which are for the most part only dimly conscious, does not achieve anything," Gebser writes, "in fact, to illuminate these states is to destroy them."[109] We should be mindful of this when we consider magical and mythical realities. When we prioritize perspectival wakefulness over unperspectival consciousness in a linear fashion of superior consciousness, there, again, is the colonization of the starry twilight worlds (and the folly of the mental is that these twilight worlds ultimately hijack the waking ego in novel ways); like lifting a rock to peer at the underworld in the light of the sun. Furthermore, to merely portray the unfoldment of the structures with the now default mentality of perspectival consciousness—in terms of gains, advancement, and progress—would be to fixate them into spatial reality (where the structures become refashioned as stages and placed higher, or lower, in a developmental ladder).

109 Gebser, *EPO*, 99.

If the archaic is a zero, the magic a point, the mythic a circle, and the mental a triangle, then the integral is expressed by a *sphere*. The characteristic of the integral structure is not twilight darkness, soulful luminosity, or daylight wakefulness, but a *transparent* lucidity capable of seeing through all dimensionalities and time forms (it should be noted that by seeing, I am using the word loosely: neither unperspectival nor perspectival seeing but another kind of spiritual sight). Space is no longer empty of value or opaque as it is in the perspectival world but full and transparent. Integrality, then, is the fully expressed and innate *wholeness* of all the mutations. It sees through to the spiritual reality that substantiates all worlds and all time forms: the ever-present reality of origin (*die Ursprung*).

This capacity—of seeing through the structures—is what allows the past and the future to become present and therefore it is a diaphanous present.[110] The integral structure thus deflates our modern compulsion towards characteristic mental abstraction (or indeed *any* structure in a state of deficient exaggeration), restored by the clarifying lucidity of originary presence.

To be integral starts, then, with presence.

We move from the dreaming of the unperspectival

110 Ibid.,102.

structures to the wakefulness of the perspectival, mental structure, and now to the *clarity* of the aperspectival, integral world. "Clarity.... is adequate, for it alone is free of brightness, twilight, and darkness, and is able to penetrate the whole where somnolent timelessness, somnial temporicity, and mental conceptuality all become diaphanous."[111] It is through this diaphaneity that all past structures become co-present to us again:

> The diaphanon, then, cannot be classed either as a form of symbolism or as a methodology; it is neither psychic nor mental, nor does it bear the stamp of magic. Rather, becoming co-visible in and through man it attests to the new mutation by which all previous spatio-temporal unfolding represented by the increments of dimensioning in consciousness are made "meaningful."[112]

Gebser gives us three important characteristics of the new mutation from which all subsequent discussion will explore. These are:

1) Temporics - "All endeavors to concretize time"

111 Ibid., 292.
112 Ibid., 135.

2) Diaphaneity - "Perceptible only in a 'world' where the concretion of time transforms time into time freedom and thus makes possible the concretion of the spiritual"

3) Verition - "the integral 'a-waring' or perception and importation 'of truth,' is the realization form of the integral consciousness structure which lends to the aperspectival world a transparent reality"[113]

The next chapter will help us move into a more detailed exploration of the leap from the perspectival mental to the aperspectival integral world.

We are still in this leap, or rather I should say that *this leap is still in us.*

It is important to "take time" with this "intra-structural" space because it is our own world, where the new and the old, the deficient mental and efficient integral are both at play in a Janus-faced mixture. For now we should simply keep in mind that the human being is the integrality of their mutations, and that to begin to leap into the integral world, we must further address time.

The preliminary task for the integral world is the concretion of time.

---

113   Ibid., 300.

We must, like Petrarch, be willing to break forth into a new reality: space has been wrought to its uttermost, and mentation has succumbed to its own leaden and fixed rationality. Therefore, for the integral to arrive, we must discover what it means to be space-free and time-free, which, for Gebser, is learning to be ego-free.

So, let us venture into the integral world and discover what that means.

6

The Integral A-Perspectival World: Time-Freedom and its Contemporary Manifestations

> *"Much of what goes on today is a dissolution; but it is not just a dissolution, for 'dissolution' also contains a 'solution.'"*[1]

> *"Our present consciousness is one of transition... the term 'irruption' signifies both the intrusion as well as the collapse for our consciousness."*[2]

Speeding to the Present

With our understanding of Gebser's concept of time—as a fourth dimensional "time freedom" where,

1 Gebser, *EPO*, 280.
2 Ibid, 284.

like the god Shiva, it manifests as a "multi-armed" or *amensional* reality—we can finally recognize why the perspectival world would have so much trouble with it. "Like any suppressed force," Gebser writes, "when first released it overpowers, frightens, and confuses us in a destructive manner."[3] Time has broken forth, and broken free. The achronon, time freedom, is ever-present origin.

Consciousness "moves" towards its intrinsic wholeness. We have been roused to wakefulness in the mental, but in the integral we are being initiated into the lucidity of origin. This is an immense, or rather we should say, immeasurable spiritual task: to not only fathom but concretize the spiritual whole. It is to allow origin to become realized *in* and *through* us. In this move from pyramidal and spatial thought to aspatial, and *spherical* relation, the world—time and space—become transparent to us. Objects no longer remain categorically flattened but become mysteriously open and diaphanous, shifting from points of dialectical opposition on a spatial plane to weird and wondrous expanses—singularities—arising in networked relation; in interbeing. The perspectival event horizon no longer remains the "vanishing point" for the ego but an aperspectival bridge

3 Ibid, 286.

between the invisible and visible and the domains that extend beyond the scope of the waking mind.

Because the spatializing mental age initiates this new mutation through systemization but cannot concretize it, a crisis of consciousness is induced: categorical maps burst and swell with the burden of complexity, the achronon shatters temporal linearity by manifesting as an exponential and runaway force. "The energy of time-freedom flares up into consciousness as an overwhelming power of time."[4] This crisis is essential for us to examine because it is the age in which we find ourselves. Just as the mythical structure helped us to understand the emergence of the soul and the eventual coming of the ego in the mental, the mental age can help us understand the emergence of time freedom and ego freedom in the integral mutation.

Gebser points out three phases in which time enters and destabilizes the perspectival world: the breaking forth of time, time irruption, and time concretion. The *breaking forth of time* occurs to us when we are not yet aware of what the phenomenon is; it appears to be happening *to* us. *Time irruption* is experienced as the increasing consciousness of time as it irrupts in our cultural phenomenology; the concept of time, clock time

4 Ibid, 360.

and anxiety, time as a force that is speeding up and out of control. Lastly, *time concretion* is the manifestation of time as an acute phenomenon in our lives, freed—at least, partially—from the spatial abstractions of the mental and expressed as a tangible presence and reality. Like any good integral phenomenon, these three phases do not happen in strict linear sequence but all at once; i.e., from all sides. The Janus-faced nature of our intra-structural moment reveals chaotic bifurcation points where the old fuses dangerously with the new:

> Since a restructuration of our form of realization is now taking place, all of its manifestations are "Janus-faced." On the one hand they are still bound to the consciousness structure in force until now which, to the extent that it is deficient, is now threatening to collapse. Yet they are already indebted to the new yet only gradually emerging consciousness structure, which is in process of formation. As a consequence a certain confusion comes to the fore because of the weakened foundations of the old manner of thinking are not yet sufficiently counterbalanced by the consolidations of the new mode of perception.[5]

5 Ibid, 280.

In these explosive admixtures the deficient mental consciousness becomes intoxicated by the dazzling novelties of efficient insight (in our case, the concretion of time and the incipient integral consciousness). Tomorrow's promise becomes today's hubris, and creative mutations becomes assimilated—even arrested and absorbed—by the all-quantifying ratio which assumes itself as the sole arbiter of the new (recall the Greek myth of the titan Kronos devouring his children). Promise and peril feed into one another in the Möbius strip of becoming. In our time of speed and extinction, technological rapidity and ecological collapse, time is breaking *up*, breaking *in*, and concretizing all at once.

The Machine and Revolution

In the first manifestation, *the breaking forth of time*, time is announced by the historically synchronous events of the industrial revolution and the awakening of the Left. Gebser asks us to look specifically to the steam engine, invented by James Watt in 1782, as the first indicator of time breaking forth into consciousness: "The machine, in the form of the steam engine, is the progenitrix of motor forces that rent asunder the static, spatial construction that had been attained since 1500."[6] Motoricity, specifically _uncontrolled_ motoricity is the key characteristic here. We make our machines (recall the links between _make_ and _magic_) yet we are possessed by the same compulsion to make them. This is McLuhan's insight that we have become, "the sex organs of the machine world, as the bee of the plant world, enabling it to fecundate and to evolve ever new forms."[7] The historical rush of exponential innovation that characterizes modernity is a manifestation of time breaking forth, but also time irruption. Modernity's symptomatic anxiety surrounding the loss of control through increasing motoricity and frenetic technological and economic advancement reaches a fever pitch in sociologist Zygmunt Bauman's "liquid modernity." Techno-philosopher Kevin Kelly recognized this trend in the early 1990s with his appropriately titled book, _Out of Control: The New Biology of Machines, Social Systems, and the Economic World,_ or more recently in _What Technology Wants._ In the latter text, Kelly posits that technology _acts as if it were a force of nature_—a "seventh" kingdom of life with its own desires and agencies—labeling it the "technium."[8] While there is

---

6 Ibid., 301.

7 McLuhan, _Understanding Media_, 46.

8 See Kevin Kelly, _What Technology Wants_ (New York: Penguin, 2010).

no room here to delve deeply into Kelly's approach, it is a fascinating confirmation of Gebser's time-irruption continuing to occur in the digital age. Ray Kurzweil has elevated time irruption into an eschatological and transhumanist principle with his prophetic exclamation of a technological singularity: through the advancement of artificial intelligence, machines will succeed the human species and become the next evolutionary leap. These technologists are intuiting what mystics like Sri Aurobindo or Teilhard de Chardin expressed a century ago, but do so through the hyper materialism of the Information Age. We are better off suggesting these mechanistic theories of the future are symptomatic manifestations of the new consciousness, literalizations that are true insofar as they are seen through to their integral, mutational theme.

Just as the machine was emancipated from its maker, the Left awakened into Western consciousness through the French Revolution (which first began in 1789, not long after the invention of the steam engine). Gebser connects these two historical events as expressing the same mutational quality. The left, as we mentioned, has hitherto in Western culture been the subject of repression and denial by the very prejudice of the mental's wakeful consciousness. The resurgence of everything that has been regarded as left—whether they are repressed individuals and cultures, women in patriarchy, human beings and the biosphere in industrial capitalism, or even (and especially) altered states of consciousness—all comes roaring back in an "uncontrolled intensity,"[9] demanding our attention. The Jewish philosopher Walter Benjamin—a contemporary of Gebser during World War II, and who tragically committed suicide in Spain while fleeing from the Nazis—expresses the intensity of the Left's consciousness best when he wrote, "the tradition of the oppressed teaches us that the "state of emergency" in which we live is not the exception but the rule."[10] Considering that Gebser understood the "supersession of patriarchy," as well as "the renunciation of dominance and power" two important qualifiers for the imminent consciousness realization, we can recognize the arising of the left into consciousness is not the signal of modernity nor even postmodernity, alone but an unfinished spiritual intensification that belongs to tomorrow as well.[11]

These two images come together: *the roaring forward of the machine world* and *the awakening of the Left*

9   Gebser, *EPO*, 262.

10 Walter Benjamin, *Illuminations* (New York: Shocken Books, 2007), 257.

11 Gebser, *EPO*, 362.

are the complimentary manifestations of time irruption. Both are concerned with emancipation: for the machine, it is an "emancipated instrument," free from our mental control even as we make it (and we are *ever* so possessed by the act of making machines). For the Left, it is the individual standing in for the whole that seeks their freedom.[12]

When we consider Gebser's insights on the early cultural phenomena of the aperspectival world—connecting everything from surrealism and Dada to Freudian psychotherapy—it is as if a pressured lid has burst open: the unconscious, time, art, technology, politics, ecology, magic, and revolution all burst forth into modern consciousness, demanding integration, and making history as we know it.

Divine Wind, Modern Angel

We should return to Walter Benjamin for a moment to illustrate not only the breaking forth of time but its irruption; time as a concept and a force breaking in and relentlessly speeding up the spatial world. In his famous essay of philosophical fragments, "Theses on the Philosophy of History," Benjamin writes about an

12 Ibid., 305.

artist who was mutually appreciated by Gebser—Paul Klee—and his painting "Angelus Novus." The painting depicts one of Klee's uniquely spectral angels gazing ahead with open wings. "This is how one pictures the angel of history,"[13] Benjamin writes, his interpretation reflecting modernity's hapless relationship with time and technology. Klee depicts time as an unstoppable divine wind blowing in from paradise:

> His face is turned toward the past. Where we perceive a chain of events, he sees one single catastrophe which keeps piling wreckage upon wreckage and hurls it in front of his feet. The angel would like to stay, awaken the dead, and make whole what has been smashed. But a storm is blowing from Paradise; it has got caught in his wings with such violence that the angel can no longer close them. This storm irresistibly propels him into the future to which his back is turned, while the pile of debris before him grows skyward. This storm is what we call progress.[14]

There is much that can be written about concerning Benjamin's Talmudic Angel of History, but a few

13 Benjamin, *Illuminations*, 257.
14 Ibid.

notable lines are relevant to our discussion of time (if we may, an exegesis of Benjamin's exegesis). The angel sees history not as a linear sequence but what we might call an *integral catastrophe*; the linearity of modernity's march towards the future is rather seen as a collapse of the mental consciousness. Time rushes forward as a great and divine storm, but it is time as it has manifested *only* through the lens of the perspectival world—an unmastered force piling up the wreckages of history "skyward" like an industrial tower. It has yet to be met with an intensification of consciousness that could master it. Benjamin's interpretation of Klee's painting acutely expresses the existential dread of twentieth century modernity's relationship to the phenomenon of time irruption (and, if we might add, our *own* moment as we face the crisis of climate change and capitalism in the Anthropocene). If we recall Gebser's commentary on how progress is a progression *away* from origin, then the angel's desire to "make whole what has been smashed," to return to origin, is a wishful interim between the archaic and the integral—strung between the two in the late mental age we perceive our reality as furthest from a participatory cosmos we have ever been. Yet, hopefully, the integral age is also most imminent.

Benjamin's interpretations here, while vivid and evoking, are also gloomy and even fatalistic. We should remember, however, that Benjamin himself was writing this passage in 1940, shortly before he took his own life, and that the conditions in Europe were indeed very grim for millions. Yet Benjamin so precisely invokes the crisis of the deficient mental consciousness and modernity here—those forces which we thought we controlled only reveal their unknowability, and furthermore, their apparent limitless intensity as they blow in as a divine wind from heaven. The mental epoch, as we have been saying (for its importance bears a continued reminder), can merely initiate the integral, but not master it. Benjamin's angel of history is an image of the irruption of time.

Integral Singularities

Perhaps the divine wind blowing in from paradise need not be a catastrophic, or rather, catastrophe itself can be apperceived from the integral structure as metamorphosis. What appears as a destructive force to us is really our own refusal to leap from a perspectively narrow field of linear time to the amensional and visionary state where time is concretized into the spiritual and manifold whole. In this state, crisis becomes integral to mutation in the process of becoming. The relationship between signal and noise, collapse and transformation, as William Irwin Thompson writes, "is at once symbiotic, like life and death, and relativistic, like time and space."[15] Yet what we are being called to do in this time is to find a way to turn noise into signal, and embrace crisis as a catalyst for a mutational leap into the future. We must continuously ask ourselves: what is catastrophe telling us? It may be that only through mysticism's *via negativa*—in our case a contemplation of catastrophic bifurcation—that we can begin to ascertain the signal through the noise and therefore the planetary cultures of the future. Pierre Teilhard de Chardin understood this when he wrote about the same winds of progress not as catastrophe alone, but as the secret forces of a divine evolution:

> Blessed be you, mighty matter, irresistible march of evolution, reality ever newborn; you who, by constantly shattering our mental categories, force us ever further and further in our pursuit of truth.

> Blessed be you, universal matter, immeasurable time, boundless ether, triple abyss of stars and atoms and generations: you who by overflowing and

dissolving our narrow standards or measurement reveal to us the dimensions of God.[16]

The challenge for us as integral thinkers is to hold both Benjamin and Teilhard in mind when we are thinking of catastrophe, transformation, and evolution all happening at once. Gebser's complex insights into Janus-faced mutational periods is helpful for this precise reason. So let us look at our second, more contemporary example of time irruption to illustrate our predicament from the mental to the integral—a *via negativa* path which forces all deficient structures into crisis, and which seems to be crying out with the planetary invocation: *leap!* Perhaps this planetary myth will help us gain the mutational confidence to do so.

* * *

Gebser describes the crisis of time irruption in the mental world as a, "frenzied rush, pushing ever outward the boundaries of the microcosm as well as of the macrocosm, dissolving—indeed destroying—and exploding rather than overcoming the spatial struc-

---

16   Pierre Teilhard de Chardin, *Hymn of the Universe* (New York: Perennial, 1972), 66.

ture."[17] For the late philosopher Paul Virilio, the signature of technological modernity is in its *dromology*—its speed.[18] Imagine a motorcycle racing down
a superhighway of the future, traveling so fast it becomes a streak of light zipping into the horizon which
is not the stars—not the sky above—but the electric
lights of the megacity below. The city is "Neo-Tokyo,"
and this is *Akira*. This 1988 Japanese film, directed by
Katsuhiro Otomo and based on the same-titled man-
ga series, was one of the first anime films that struck
a resonant cord in Western culture, humming with the
same edgy "technical vitalism"[19] (another appropriate
Virilio term) of what was then an emerging literary and
cinematic genre of cyberpunk, popularized by William
Gibson's *Neuromancer* or Ridley Scott's *Blade Runner*.
Akira is suffused with a kind of primal power—and
mutational urgency—in everything from its entranc-
ing percussive soundtrack to its depiction of a hypertrophied post-apocalyptic industrialism. Foreboding
chants annunciate the coming of a new consciousness for our anti-hero, Tetsuo, a young member of a

17 Gebser, EPO, 353.

18 See Paul Virilio, *Speed and Politics* (Los Angeles: Semiotext(e),
2007).

19 Ibid.

Neo-Tokyo biker gang who during a high-speed chase crashes his bike into a child with psychic powers. As Virilio notes, *speed* is the signature note of the machine's power, but when we invented the automobile we also invented the *crash*.[20]

As Tetsuo recovers from the accident, he realizes that the crash—and the child who was fleeing from a secret government lab—unlocked some new, psychic mutation in himself. We learn that old Tokyo was destroyed during World War III, not by a *nuclear* attack but a *psychic* bomb. Akira, another test subject from the military science lab, was involved in a catastrophic accident that leveled Tokyo to the ground through a terrifying psychic implosion: a mental singularity. His remains, like an Egyptian pharaoh, were placed by scientists in glass urns and hidden in a vault deep in the subterranean layers of the city.

The film asks: what would a bacterial cell do if it suddenly mutated and gained the consciousness of a human being? By the same measure, what would a human being do if it achieved some vast, evolutionary leap into super consciousness? Would we be able to

---

20 See John David Ebert, *The Age of Catastrophe: Disaster and Humanity in Modern Times* (Jefferson: McFarland, 2012), vi. Paul Virilio asks: "How could we manage to analyze today's technical progress if we don't analyze its accidents?"

wield such power without destroying ourselves? Towards the end of the film, Tetsuo has completely lost control of his newfound power. While fighting against the military, and his friend Kaneda, he has regenerated his arm through a body-horror assemblage of wires and machine detritus. His new arm writhes like a band of snakes—all mesh and wire—seeming to have a will of its own, and hinting to us that Tetsuo's powers are truly out of control (a motif echoed in the 1989 cyberpunk horror film *Tetsuo: The Iron Man*). In the movie's finale—certainly infamous in cinema history for its shocking body horror—Tetsuo's hypertrophied ego cannot contain his consciousness mutation any longer. He inflates, like a dying star, into what looks like a giant baby; flesh oozes like an octopus out of water, and tentacled arms writhe about in all directions. Tetsuo cries for help. He is at last undone by his own power. At this scene one thinks of Kubrick's parallel film *2001: A Space Odyssey* and David Bowman's Star Child, but Tetsuo has yet to make the evolutionary leap into the new consciousness. However, just like Bowman, Tetsuo has an evolutionary midwife who makes an appearance and guides him through to the other side of the singularity. Akira materializes just in time to take Tetsuo into a new dimension (it is worth noting that the boy, Akira, is depicted as a luminescent and *transparent* human body).

The city of Neo-Tokyo is saved, and the final scene moves us through to a cosmic light—perhaps another Big Bang—with Tetsuo's voice exclaiming from the void in cosmic jubilee, "I am Tetsuo."

As a film, *Akira* functions as what William Irwin Thompson describes as a "planetary mythology,"[21] a singular distillation of what is happening collectively in consciousness and culture—like Gebser's image of the crowned Prince of Krete so perfectly expressing the move from the magic to the mythic. Perhaps like no other film, *Akira* concretizes the Janus-faced ambiguity of the perspectival world and its unleashing of time—the upending and overwhelming energy of the integral achronon—as a power that cannot be mastered either by the hypertrophied ego or the spatializing mental. Tetsuo was intoxicated by the powers unleashed within him, but from the initial elation of ego in its frenzy of self-aggrandizement follows its over-extension and demise. The mutation happening to Tetsuo like the new integral realization in our own world, bursts out of such restrictions, and manifests as an animating and speeding force—Virilio's dromology. The new consciousness, when not consciously integrated, manifests as an increasing intensity upon the

21 Thompson, *Passages About Earth*, 119.

old. The old, rather than being consciously overcome, becomes unconsciously overwhelmed.

The image of Neo-Tokyo, with its runaway forces of technological evolution, time irruption, and consciousness intensification, is an image of our world—a myth concerning the birth of planetary culture and the *homo integer*.

Time Freedom and the Spiritual Implications of Integral Consciousness

We have looked at the mental age intermixing with the integral, but what does time begin to look like as we move away from the interim age and begin to consider Gebser's time-as-presence?

Time irruption is an integral phenomenon and announces the coming of time itself, not as clock time but as time's quintessence: its fourth dimensionality. This form of time, to the paradoxical surprise of many of us still anchored in the mental world, is *time-freedom*. In the mental structure time is still the divider, and so long as we continue to perceive it his way it will *go on* dividing, disrupting, and separating space. Yet as Gebser says: "what is prepared for is more than a mere concept of 'time'; it is the achronon, or time freedom, a freedom and liberation from every temporal form."[22]

What does it mean that time *is* time freedom? The statement sounds vaguely conceptual, like another science fiction film (and, no surprise, science fiction is an excellent genre to explore the concept of time as it morphs and mutates within popular consciousness), yet as Gebser clearly asserts—and as the previous chapters have hopefully demonstrated—there is so much *latent* in the present that cannot be reduced to a mere *now*. Presence is not a singular moment split apart into a thousand, fragmented "nows." Instead, presence reveals time's multiplicity: "the undivided presence of yesterday, today, and tomorrow which in a consciously realized actualization can lead to that 'presentiation' which encompasses origin as an ineradicable presence."[23] This would mean that the future is *here* with us just as much as the past.

What kind of intensified consciousness needs to "come online" to experience presence in this way? What kind of intensified reality do we need step into? To make it palpable—embodied—rather than an admittedly fascinating but abstract concept? For Gebser this consciousness is a move from abstraction to

22   Gebser, *EPO*, 284.
23   Ibid., 294.

concretion, and if there is any practice for us looking
to integrate this insight into our lives, it is the contemplative's life; not necessarily the monastic contemplative, but one who is present with presence as a means
to bring forth the integral human being as we live
through climate change and civilizational catastrophe.
It is a form of presence that Gebser invokes when quoting Friedrich Hölderlin: "Behold! it is the eve of time,
the hour when the wanderers turn toward their resting
place. One god after another is coming home... Therefore, be present."[24] For the integral scholar, I believe it
is also a kind of sympathetic presence with the world,
a re-tuning of the magical structure's labyrinthine ear
for integral temporics. Gebser demonstrated a natural
capacity for being present in his study of language, art,
and other forms of cultural expression; his presence allowed him to "tune" into the underlying phenomenology of consciousness at work in each structure. It is this
act of sympathetic presence that we can take with us
into the future, allowing us to continue Gebser's work
in the twenty-first century without simply mimicking
the conceptual framework of the archaic, magic, mythic, mental, and integral terminology. We should only
use these concepts if they are *more* than mere concepts,

24 Ibid., 102.

but phenomenologically encountered realities.

Receptivity and lucidity are the qualities that one should be working towards, if it can be said there is something to spatially work *towards* anymore in this structure (after all, the *sphericity* of the integral world implies that, rather than a working towards, we attempt a seeing through, a relating to the whole and sustaining ourselves in the whole). When we become present we cultivate the capacity for openness; what "shines" forth in this openness is all that we have been and all that we will become, not merely as individuals but also in the "longer" view: the structures of consciousness, genetic and evolutionary ancestry, and cosmic being. It is through only openness and spaciousness that we can become present to these things latent *in* presence, and capable of co-enacting the infinite and creative powers of origin. It is through this diaphaneity that we become co-conscious "mutants" for the future; mutations as leaps of consciousness are done when we have moved *with* that which moves *us* into new realizations of being. In this vastness everything becomes transparent. Here everything dynamically speaks to and informs itself as it manifests both as an ego in time and a cosmic whole that wares through time. Indeed, Gebser concluded *Ever Present Origin* with, "in truth we ware the whole and the whole wares us."[25]

This is what we find in presence: the unity of past and future, the consciously attained presence of spiritual origin. What cannot be conceptually pinned down can be a-rationally wared, or seen through.

The word, *a* (free) and *chronon* (time) implies that a new spiritual freedom is attained in the integral mutation, yet we should be careful not to disregard the achievements of each of the structures of consciousness. The magical's *one*, the mythical's *two*, and the mental's *three* dimensionalities are each and all retained and become, as it were, superconscious. "We perceive the world in its foundations are not exclusively bound,"[26] Gebser writes, to any one of the structures. Fixity is superseded. This time freedom is a new dimensionality we enter into, or rather, the "amension,"[27] and thus capable of waring all dimensionalities and integrating them beyond the fixed capacities of the mental's synthesizing mind; through this direct waring, Gebser's concept of *verition* comes into play, a kind of mutual imparting of truth, that is, the transparent, aperspectival

25 Ibid., 543.
26 Ibid., 356.
27 Ibid.

reality.[28] If an integral understanding "from all sides," systasis, becomes our method, then this moves us into something altogether different from mental synthesis. Instead, we begin to have *synairesis*, which we might describe summarily here as an expression of the whole. Time freedom, then, is both the quintessence of time *and* the quintessence of every singularly unique time form expression:

> To the perception of the aperspectival world time appears to be the very fundamental function, and to be of a most complex nature. It manifests itself in accordance with a given consciousness structure and the appropriate possibility of manifestation in its various aspects as clock time, natural time, cosmic or sidereal time; as biological duration, rhythm, meter; as mutation, discontinuity, relativity; as vital dynamics, psychic energy (and thus in a certain sense in the form we call "soul" and the "unconscious"), and as mental dividing. It manifests itself as the unity of past, present, and future; as the creative principle, the power of imagination, as work, and even as "motoricity." And along with the vital, psychic, biological, cos-

28 Ibid., 300.

mic, rational, creative, sociological, and technical aspects of time, we must include—last but not least—psychical-geometric time which is designated as the "fourth dimension.[29]

Similarly, Gebser leaves us with a descriptive, rather than a prescriptive list of integral qualities. This list is in no particular order, but it expresses some of the important characteristics of the new mutation. The general 3-points for integral phenomena (mentioned in the previous chapter) of temporics, diaphaneity, and verition "show up" in this list of criteria in their varying forms: temporics, for instance, through the realization of timelessness, or time-freedom, and diaphaneity and verition through the spiritual. These integral qualities can manifest through individuals and whatever their particular styles of cultural expression might be—poetic, linguistic, scientific, or otherwise. In Part Two of *Ever-Present Origin*, Gebser meticulously searches for these integral signifiers as they manifested across trans-disciplinary fields (literature, social science, physics, history, economics, and religion to name a few). We will leave it to the reader to investigate these developments for themselves and draw the necessary

29 Ibid.

connections between the 1940s and the 2010s. This helpful list can assist us in waring the integral reality making its appearance in our own moment of cultural evolution:

> the whole,
> integrity,
> transparency (diaphaneity)
> the spiritual (the diaphainon)
> the supersession of the ego,
> the realization of timelessness,
> the realization of temporicity,
> the realization of the concept of time,
> the realization of time-freedom (the achronon),
> the disruption of the merely systematic,
> the incursion of dynamics,
> the recognition of energy,
> the mastery of movement,
> the fourth dimension,
> the supersession of patriarchy,
> the renunciation of dominance and power,
> the acquisition of intensity,
> clarity (instead of mere wakefulness),
> and the transformation of the creative inceptual basis[30]

30   Ibid., 362.

As Gebser writes, "these key terms presuppose the overcoming, or at least an attempt at overcoming, certain 'isms'... perspectivism; dualism; dialectics; positivism; nihilism; existentialism; pragmatism; psychism; vitalism; mechanism; rationalism; and spiritism, to name only a few."[31] What makes any and all overcoming of "isms" possible is the temporics of the aperspectival world; time freed from its mental conception and arrayed in its full amensionality through the integral consciousness. This helps us to appreciate the task we are given—towards the "new statement"—made possible by the aforementioned descriptors.[32] In Gebser's careful navigation of language, he is attempting to bring the work itself closer to an integral form of statement. Rather than merely abstract integral consciousness into a concept, it is language itself that becomes Gebser's underlying concern in the nature of his communication: can a work about the integral structure also be an integral expression? This is what makes Gebser's writing, even in translation, so evocative: it achieves a form of literary integrality—the mutual imparting of the integral reality in the reading and the reader, producing an intensified clarity and presence

31 Ibid.
32 Ibid., 361.

in the text regardless of its perceived mental difficul-
ty. For us—writing and reading across time—we are
given a challenge to continue to "lean into" the task of
presentiating the diaphanous world. This is synonymous with leaning into the future. For both the artist
and the scholar—or the artist-scholar, the producer of
Wissenkunst[33]—the task is to produce not only an intensification of consciousness in ourselves but in those
who we reach through what we have made.[34]

Gebser reminds us that systasis and synairesis help
us to "bring together what is not three-dimensionally
comprehensible," and so these integral concepts assist
us as we begin to familiarize ourselves with temporics.
It is worth examining one final quote at length concerning time-freedom, as it helps us to comprehend our moment of critical choice between leaping into the future

33 William Irwin Thompson, *The Time Falling Bodies Take to Light:
    Mythology, Sexuality and the Origins of Culture* (New York: Saint
    Martin's Press, 1996), 4.

34 Gebser's unique challenge remains a careful balancing act: we
    should not seek to completely avoid the mental conceptualization
    (the dialectic) or the mythical narrative (for instance, the struc-
    tures of consciousness could be conveyed as a separation from
    and return to Origin), but instead attempt new forms of integral
    statement to impart and express a waring of wholeness and the
    integrality of the evolutionary process—past, present, and fu-
    ture. This is not so much post-dialectical, or post-mythical, as a
    new line of flight and a new challenge of integral concept (veri-
    tion).

or (for lack of a better phrase) the future taking us for a leap. "Time-freedom is the conscious form of archaic, original pre-temporality,"[35] meaning origin—the Itself, the very spiritual and creative principle—becomes conscious in the human being. What happens when we are no longer perspectively bound to the mental world? Everything vast and ancient in time (and their respective time forms) moves to the forefront—from hominids to Lascaux to Kukulkan—not threatening to overwhelm us but restored to their presence as worlds, singularities; unique expressions of consciousness, time, space, and being. What is latent in the future also looms in the present. The future is available to presence through a clarity that the linear ego is woe to comprehend but the greater, transparent self-consciousness—for an integral human being is a *whole* human being—has the capacity to ware. Gebser writes:

> By granting to magic timelessness, mythical temporicity, and mental-conceptual temporality their integral efficacy, and by living them in accord with the strength of their degree of consciousness, we are able to bring about this realization. The concretion of the previous three exfolia-

35 Gebser, *EPO*, 356.

tions of original pre-temporality instantaneously opens for us pre-conscious timelessness.

As such, time-freedom is not only the quintessence of time... but also the conscious quintessence of all previous time forms. Their becoming conscious—in itself a process of concretion—is also a liberation from al these time forms; everything becomes present, concrete, and thus integrable present. But this implies that preconscious origins becomes conscious present; that each and every time-form basic to one-, two-, and three-dimensional world is integrated and thereby superseded.[36]

Since fixity towards any one of the structures is relaxed in the integral realization, a gentle *de-centering* of the mental consciousness takes place; all time forms arise and are co-present. Whatever is needed in response to a particular crisis or challenge is capable of springing forth in creative participation with origin. This immanental presence is no longer a point or a triad but the sphere. In a sphere, whether something is near or far is not a matter of distance but of attention. This is what "seeing through the world" really means

36 Ibid.

for us. As we begin to face the prospect of our own extinction through the sixth mass extinction event in Earth's deep evolutionary time, it is as if the whole of who we are, have been, and could be all have come to the forefront of our consciousness and let us truly *see* ourselves for the first time. This mutational crisis can, we hope, be a gift and a catalyst. After all, what is the kind of self-consciousness apprehended from this long evolutionary view? Suffice to say that this intensified waring is the beginning of Teilhard's planetization.

We are more than the mental self, and for those sensitive enough, the structures of consciousness can open up to us so that *other selves* may speak. The type of thinking needed for survival in the Anthropocene— when the sheer mass of global industrial civilization under capitalism is leaving a geological "footprint" on the Earth—is a certain diaphanous perceiving of the more-than-human world, and we are gratefully seeing this shift (at least) in the humanities through the ecological interest in the "non-human turn" (recognizing the agency and subjectivity of other than-human organisms, or even other-than-human entities from rocks to tools to mountains). Ecological thinking *is* aperspectival; it is an understanding of complex systems, but these systems are not "merely systematic." Time-freedom reveals the deep interplay, an "incursion of dynamics" between human beings and the rest of the biosphere.

Philosophy begins to concern itself with the limits of reason, and academics begin to peek their heads out on the other side of the rational, labeling it the "world without us" (as Eugene Thacker has helpfully coined).[37] Meanwhile, other thinkers have begun to abandon the perspectival world of Kantian objects with schools of thought such as Object Oriented Ontology (OOO), an intriguing development from the philosopher Graham Harman; in aperspectival style, spatial consciousness irrupts with the uncanny, and perspectival objects are decoupled from their reductive utility as exhaustible pieces of matter (tools and terms) that can be measured. Objects become strange and occluded—like a Renaissance painting morphing into some form of Impressionism—unknowable, withdrawn from fixity. Yet this occlusion is in actuality a *diaphaneity*. Objects burst from the confines of mental space and become unfathomable singularities, each thing an opening to the strange and wondrous inward skies of Rilke's poetry.

Finally, in these qualities we have the move from the mental ego to the integral self. The perspectival

---

37 See Eugene Thacker, *In The Dust of This Planet* (Alesford: Zero Books, 2011)

ego is just the beginning of what we understand to be self-consciousness; it is the integral self that stands in for the whole and represents an intensified self-perception. It is *you* who had burst out into the magical nexus of the animal world with imagination, attuning yourself to the starry cosmogony in the acoustic caves, and *you* who now bursts forth as an avatar of electric light in the technological surround of the twenty-first century, crashing upon the brimmed edge of disaster and wonder. It is, hopefully, in this waring *through* to our origins that we can realize that *all* phases of our genesis—yesterday, today, and tomorrow—are dynamically ever-present and inform our planetary becoming. This is some inkling of the integral self. This is the kind of self capable of inheriting the future.

It is through the archaic integrality of consciousness that we have always acted, and it is through the conscious presence of origin that we must now continue to act from, in primal trust.

Primal Trust

In a talk hosted in 1972, "Primal Fear and Primal Trust," Gebser considers this inquiry of origin ("Where do I come from?," "Who am I?," and "Whither do I go?")³⁸ as a singularly important set of questions concerning the integral human being:

> So long as we do not find an answer to those questions, primal fear reigns. From it springs, to the degree that we become aware of those questions, the diverse creaturely, psychic, and intellectual anxieties. It is also in the last analysis the trigger for aggression and depression... which can lead to the destruction of others or of oneself. Only he who finds an answer to these questions awakens primal trust and thus is freed from primal fear. What is most incomprehensible is that in this case he will have overcome the primal fear forever and is therefore not threatened by any relapse into it.³⁹

In the 1960s, Gebser traveled through Asia to "put flesh on the bones"⁴⁰ of his knowledge of India and the Far East, producing *Asia Primer* in 1962 and then *Asia Smiles Differently* in 1968. It was during this trip that Gebser had his profound religious experience while visiting Sarnath, India (where the Buddha held his first sermon). It seemed to confirm a lifetime of insight—

38 Feuerstein, *Structures of Consciousness*, 30.

39 Ibid.

40 Ibid., 29.

and that first "lightning" strike of inspiration back during the 1930s. In a letter written to Georg Feuerstein in 1971, Gebser described this experience:

> It was sober, on the one hand happening with crystal clarity in everyday life, which I perceived and to which I reacted "normally," and on the other hand and simultaneously being a transfiguration and irradiation of the indescribable, unearthly, transparent "Light"—no ecstasy, no emotion, but a spiritual clarity, a quiet jubilation, a knowledge of invulnerability, a primal trust... Since Sarnath I am as if recast, inwardly, since then everything is in its proper place—and it continues to take effect and is in a way an irradiation that is always present and at hand.[41]

This experience happened in 1961, and it is testament to the "invulnerability" of such a primal trust that Gebser seemed profoundly changed even a decade later. While visiting D.T. Suzuki in Japan, Gebser would receive confirmation of his experience as an "instance of *satori*."[42] The qualities of this "quiet jubilation" and its

41 Ibid., 173.
42 Ibid.

transfiguration of consciousness in clarity and "transparent light" lends us further insight into the qualities of tomorrow's *homo integer*. This final criteria is an expansion of the previous list, and offered to us towards the end of Gebser's life in his final book, *Decline and Participation*:

> Haste is replaced by silence and the capacity for silence;
>
> Goal oriented, purposive thought is replaced by unintentionalness;
>
> The pursuit of power is replaced by the genuine capacity for love;
>
> Quantitative idle motion (*Leerlauf*) is replaced by the qualitative spiritual process;
>
> Manipulation is replaced by the patient acceptance of the providential powers;
>
> Mechanistic classification and organization is replaced by the "being-in-order" (*In-der-Ordnung-sein*);
>
> Prejudice is replaced by the renunciation of value judgements, that is to say, the emotional short-circuit (*Kurzschluss*) is replaced by unsentimental tolerance;
>
> Action is replaced by poise (*Haltung*);

Homo faber is replaced by *homo integer*;

The divided human being is replaced by the whole human being;

The emptiness of the limited world is replaced by the open expanse of the open world[43]

* * *

Now, time has ended; or, at least, linear time. New Media collapses past, present, and future into the digital *now*, but unless we are deeply aware of how our reliance on spiraling mental consciousness—ratio—can no longer bear the burden and energy of the achronon, time-freedom, then we will succumb to a kind of mutational stasis (or what Mark Fisher has importantly described as "Capitalist Realism," a failure to envision new realities beyond our current economic ideology).[44]

43 Ibid., 170.

44 We should note that Fisher's "Capitalist Realism" is talking about the cultural phenomenology of an ideology—capitalism—and its impact on arresting culture. Gebser was certainly not one for emphasizing economic ideologies but perhaps a certain freedom *from* ideologies. In this case, we can appreciate Fisher's Capitalist Realism as an expression of mental-ratio, a stasis. The issue with a predominantly capitalistic society is that its central ideology is the "bottom line" realism: quantification. Totalizing quantification is an indication of deficiency in any consciousness, and so we

A failure to leap into new plateaus of being as the dead weight of the past to forces time to stand still, and the world to go dark. This will not do. As one who shares a primal trust in the power of tomorrow, and the capacity of the human being to creatively realize these mutations of consciousness in themselves, I stand with Gebser in saying that the future is present and can inform us. We are not alone, nor are we lost; it is only when we remain narrowly confined to the style of thinking and mentation of the deficient consciousness that we have no future.

Gebser offers us a way of thinking about the present that is difficult to disagree with in any of its major points: the structures of consciousness are palpable realities that can be recognized by the careful reader in a concrete way, the Janus-faced interim age between the mental and the integral inform us on our current crisis between technology and the biosphere, capitalism and a future means of distributive and immanental Gaian politics. These visions of the future are what anthropologist David Graeber calls "pre-figurative,"[45] but

---

can see part of our problem, from Fukuyama's "End of History" to capitalist realism, has more to do with the underlying structure of consciousness that the ideology of capitalism adheres to.

45 See David Graeber, "Occupy Wall Street's Anarchist Roots," *Al Jazeera*: https://www.aljazeera.com/indepth/opin-

this should not stop us from experimenting with them. When we take these leaps of primal trust into the wisdom of tomorrow we are not acting on faith alone. We come from the future, and pull the present into a new potentiality. Let us make it, then, a spiritual present.

ion/2011/11/2011112872835904508.html [last accessed 28 Nov 2018].

"The simple is in us. It is participation—participation in that which is unknown yet evident to us: a tiny seed in us, which contains all transparency—the diaphanous world, the most irradiated and most sober beatitude. It is so completely comprehensive and whole that neither our intelligent, super-clever, caged-in thought nor our pitiable-pitiful and needy-strong longing—how much poverty it renders visible!—can even divine it. And yet, it is within us."

—*Jean Gebser*
April 26 1973[1]

---

1 Preface to *Verfall und Teilhabe*, trans. Georg Feuerstein, (Lower Lake: Integral Publishing, 1987), 31–32. Gebser's last literary piece, written shortly before his death on May 14, the following month (Feuerstein, 32).

Perspective	Structure	Signifier	Time Expression	Characteristic	Mode of Thought
Pre-Perspectival	Archaic	Zero	Pre-Spatial/Pre-Temporal	Innate integrality as maximum latency	
Pre-Perspectival	Magic	Point	Spaceless/Timeless	Unitary Nexus/Diffuse	
Unperspectival	Mythic	Circle	Symbolic Space/Natural Temporicity or Rhythmicity	Eternal Recurrence, Complementary Polarities	Oceanic Thinking
Perspectival	Mental	Triangle	Spatial/Abstractly Temporal	Directedness, Opposed Dualities, Spatializing	Pyramidal Thinking
Aperspectival	Integral	Sphere	Space-Free/Time-Free	Diaphanous, "rendering whole," Presence, Innate integrality realized	Verition, Systasis, and Syn-airesis

7

Integral Florilegium: Secondary Sources, Reading, Immanent Scholarship

*F*LORILEGIUM, which roughly translates from Latin to mean "a gathering of flowers," were medieval compilations of sayings from Greek philosophers and the Early Church Fathers.[1] Maria Papova, the creator of the popular literary curation site *Brainpickings*, tells us that these texts were, "essentially mashing up selected passages and connecting dots from existing texts to illuminate a specific topic or doctrine or idea," and, most importantly, that they were a prelude to what she describes as the "combinatorial creativity" and "networked knowledge" of digital remix culture.[2] For every good idea that sprouts up

1 Maria Papova. "Networked Knowledge and Combinatorial Creativity," *Brain Pickings*: www.brainpickings.org/2011/08/01/networked-knowledge-combinatorial-creativity/ [last accessed 5 Dec 2018].

2 Ibid.

on the surface of culture, there are a thousand nodes—
like a mycelial web—that had to first connect under
the surface. Popova's concepts not only help to set the
stage for this closing chapter, but are also *themselves* an
expression of aperspectival epistemology (knowledge
making).

The aperspectival subject is an assemblage: a self
realized not as hypertrophied ego—in the Western
image of the solitary genius—but as an ecology, the
network of their relations and imprints. This view of
knowledge and art making releases us from perspectival fixation (knowledge as created solely by the individual) to aperspectival relation (knowledge as flow,
assemblage, comprised not only of its visible factors
but also sustained by the invisible, spiritual whole). It
is fitting, then to conclude this text with a gathering
of integral *florilegium*—curated by myself and so by no
means exhaustive—for the reader to delve in further
for their own study of Gebser and possibly even to support varied aperspectival initiatives and projects.

Organizations

Gebser's work has influenced many diverse individuals across all fields—artists, philosophers, architects, poets, Jungian psychologists, transpersonal ther-

apists, Buddhists, indigenous wisdom holders—many of whom come together annually for the International Jean Gebser Society conferences. The Gebser Society, founded in 1980 by Algis Mickunas (who, along with Noel Barstard translated *The Ever-Present Origin* into English in 1986) in Athens, Ohio, at Ohio University, has gone on to produce decades of academic research and a number of publications in the English-speaking world, especially (but not limited to) the field of Communications. In many ways, these conferences continue in the English-speaking world what Gebser initiated with "The New Worldview" conferences, hosted consecutively in 1952 and 1953 (following the publications of *Ever-Present Origin*), and drawing from a diverse array of scholars.

Today, I am honored to serve as the society's standing president and help to organize our annual conferences, the latest of which has been 2018's "Gebser and Asia," presided at Naropa University. The Gebser Society's mission is the same today: to further integral pedagogy and to serve as something of an integral praxis—and intensive—for the conference participants (performing arts, poetry, and contemplative practices are scheduled alongside academic presentations).

Our society has published a number of anthology projects as *Diaphany* (2015), *Communications, Compara-*

tive Cultures, and Civilizations (2008, 2012, 2013), and our journal, *Integrative Explorations: Journal of Culture and Consciousness* (1999–2003, edited by Michael Purdy), and *Consciousness and Culture: An Introduction to the Thought of Jean Gebser* (1992, edited by Eric Kramer). A list of universities and Gebserian scholars can be found on our resources page.

Gebser's bibliography, biographical notes, as well as the conference archives, conference publications, and a community Listserv for the society can be found at our website: www.gebser.org. I encourage you to attend any of our forthcoming conferences, or consider presenting your own research with us.

For the German-speaking world, The European Jean Gebser Society (Integrale Weltsicht) is available. Rudolf Hammerli, the editor of Gebser's complete works (*Gesamtausgabe*, 1986/1999), is their society president. Visit their homepage here: http://www.jean-gebser-gesellschaft.ch/.

Institutions

A list of Gebserian scholars and associated universities can be found on the Gebser Society's resource page.[3] In addition to the Department of History of Science at the University of Oklahoma, the California Institute of Integral Studies remains a highly active locus point for integral scholarship. CIIS has a long history with the American consciousness culture—the "integral milieu" which took root in the United States around the mid century—and traces its roots back to Alan Watts, Frederic Spiegelberg, and Haridas Chaudhuri (*The Evolution of Integral Consciousness*, 1978). Chaudhuri was a student of Sri Aurobindo's, and so the connections with Gebser are self-evident.

A number of significant integral philosophers and scholars in the extended milieu have helped to shape CIIS as an institution and have incorporated Gebser at least partially into their work. A few can be named here, such as Robert McDermott (*Steiner and Kindred Spirits: An Introduction to Rudolf Steiner for the 21st Century*, 2009), Richard Tarnas (*Cosmos and Psyche: Intimations of a New World View*, 2006), Allan Combs (*The Radiance of Being: Understanding the Grand Integral Vision; Living the Integral Life*, 1996), Sean Kelly (*Coming Home: The Birth. & Transformation of the Planetary Era*, 2010), and Debashish Banerji (*The Seven Quartets of Becoming: A*

---

3 See "Resources." Jean Gebser Society: http://www.gebser.org/resources/ [last accessed 1 Dec 2018].

Transformative Yoga Psychology Based on the Diaries of Sri Aurobindo, 2012), Kerri Welch, PhD (Gebser Society scholar, researching the philosophy of physics, time, and mind), and Matthew David Segall, PhD (another Gebser Society scholar, researching process philosophy of Schelling and Whitehead).[4] Allan Combs also serves as president for the Society for Consciousness Studies at CIIS, which can be accessed here: https://consc.org.

Secondary Sources and Translations

Gebser's work has made its way into many different fields, but explicit, secondary English sources are exceedingly rare beyond the published works of the Gebser Society. Dr. Georg Feuerstein's *Structures of Consciousness: The Genius of Jean Gebser* (1987) is the most erudite and recommended companion to *Ever-Present Origin*. It is no longer in print, but copies may be accessed through local or university libraries or (hopefully) a reasonable price on Amazon. Feuerstein (1947–2012) was a preeminent scholar of yoga, friend and colleague of Gebser's, and longtime participant of the Gebser Society. Please see his work and the work of

---

4   See Matthew David Segall's blog and homepage. Footnotes2Plato. https://footnotes2plato.com/ [last accessed 1 Dec 2018].

Brenda Feuerstein (*Green Yoga*, 2007), who continues to publish and offer mentorship training at Traditional Yoga Studies: www.traditionalyogastudies.com.

Gebser Society scholar and translator, Aaron Cheak has published a thorough "philosophical biography" of Gebser, as well as translations of Jean Gebser's poetry (*Afternoon Poems*, 1936/44 and *The Winter Poem*, 1944) on his website.[5] Through Rubedo Press, Dr. Cheak has created The Jean Gebser Project, which aims to begin publishing "a series of dedicated translations and critical studies of Gebser's work," starting with *Rilke and Spain* (1940) and *The Grammatical Mirror* (1944).[6]

Further Reading (Inspired and Corroborative)

Revelore Press has a forthcoming anthology—in the same spirit as the Gebser Society conferences, though only creatively inspired by Gebser's concepts—called MUTATIONS: *Art, Consciousness and the Anthropocene* (2019), of which I am co-editor of with Dr. Jenn Zahrt.

---

5 Aaron Cheak, "From Poetry to Kulturphilosophie: A Philosophical Biography of Jean Gebser with Critical Translations," http://www.aaroncheak.com/from-poetry-to-kulturphilosophie [last accessed 1 Dec 2018].

6 The Jean Gebser Project: http://rubedo.press/gebser/ [last accessed 1 Dec 2018].

As we write, "By putting words to the page through literary, political, and artistic creation, we generate *instances*, *mutations*, of these new worlds—realizations of the future latent in the present."[7] Contributions range from astrology to archetypal history and media studies.

William Irwin Thompson, who has been referred to throughout this work, is a preeminent scholar of consciousness studies and has adapted some of Gebser's concepts and shares a phenomenological approach to cultural evolution. Following the publication of *At The Edge of History* (1971), Thompson formed the Lindisfarne Association (1972–2012), which, in the spirit of the aperspectival world, featured the likes of E.F. Schumacher, Francisco Varela, Brother David Steindl-Rast, Huston Smith, Lynn Margulis, Wendell Berry, Gary Snyder, Kathleen Raine, Evan Thompson, Carl Sagan, and Joan Halifax Roshi—just to name a handful.[8] For an autobiographical memoir of the Lindisfarne Association, see Thompson's *Thinking Together*

7   See our Call for Papers and Book Description. "Art, Consciousness, and the Anthropocene: A Revelore Press Anthology," https://revelore.press/publications/mutations/ [last accessed 1 Dec 2018].

8   See "Lindisfarne Tapes: A Collection of Conversations about Culture, Society, Technology and Economy," Schumacher Center for a New Economics: https://centerforneweconomics.org/envision/legacy/lindisfarne-tapes/ [last accessed 1 Dec 2018].

at the *Edge of History: A Memoir of the Lindisfarne Association, 1972–2012* (2016). *Imaginary Landscape: Making Worlds of Myth and Science* (1990) and *Coming into Being: Artifacts and Texts in the Evolution of Consciousness* (1998) both draw directly on Gebser's structures of consciousness. Kelly's aforementioned *Coming Home* makes comparative work between Gebser's structures, Thompson's cultural ecologies, and the mathematical mentalities developed by Thompson's colleague Ralph Abraham (*Bolts from the Blue: Art, Mathematics, and Cultural Evolution*, 2011); he sees Thompson's advantage over Gebser—perhaps because he was writing later, from the heart of the New Age movement in the 1970s—was linking the integral-aperspectival with the notion of planetary culture.

Ken Wilber has adapted Gebser's concepts for his own, developmentally emphasized Integral Theory. Wilber has been a popularizer of integral concepts through his widely translated works such as *A Brief History of Everything* (1996), and his theory has since become the basis of an international community of psychologists, scholars, organizational theorists (Frederic Laloux, for instance and his *Reinventing Organizations*, 2014), and think tanks (The Institute for Cultural Evolution and Integral Institute). Many integral theorists in this global community are familiar with Gebser's terminology—archaic, magic, mythic, mental, and integral—but not with Gebser's own writing (hopefully this book has been a remedy)! Integral Theory's emphasis on all-encompassing, meta systemic maps of reality is definitively a *mental* expression, according to Gebser's approach (progress-oriented and linear, even *multi*-linear, rather than mutational and structural), as well as perspectival (categorical, where *everything* has its spatial point on the map). Nevertheless, integral theorists, especially in recent years, have expressed continuing interest in alternative—and complementary—conceptions of cultural evolution. My presentation, "Meta Matrixes, Planetary Lattices and Integral A-Waring," at the 2015 Gebser Society conference, explored Wilber's spatial emphasis as a "Janus-faced" manifestation of the interim period between the mental and the integral structures.[9]

Gary Lachman—another Gebser Society scholar and author of many books on occult philosophy—has featured some of Gebser's core insights in his own theory on the evolution of consciousness in the recent comprehensive (and recommended) text, *The Secret Teachers of the Western World* (2015). John David Ebert, a cultural

---

9 See "Architects of the Integral World," Jean Gebser Society: http://www.gebser.org/2015-program-1 [last accessed 1 Dec 2018].

philosopher, has written a number of Gebser-inspired texts, which we have cited in this book (*The New Media Invasion: Digital Technologies and the World the Unmake*, 2011). Gebser scholar Glenn Aparicio Parry has written *Original Thinking: A Radical Revisioning of Time, Humanity, and Nature* (2015), which explores the evolution of Western thought in dialogue between Native American elders and scientists. Finally, Daniel Pinchbeck's *2012: The Return of Quetzalcoatl* (2007), which helped to catalyze a new wave of consciousness culture, brought Gebser's insights on time to the forefront of cultural discussion on the need for re-integration of the mythical and magical time expressions.

Foundational Books

A few key texts are likely to be necessary for the integral scholar to acclimate to Gebser's highly unique expression of temporics: Henri Bergson's *Creative Evolution* (1907) and *Matter and Memory* (1896) are both significant here, not as mere stepping stones or precursors to integral thinking but for their profound insights *on* integral thinking; indeed, on the exploration of time itself (it should be noted that Bergson was more central for Teilhard's writings). It would be Deleuze who would revive Bergsonism in the late twentieth century and so, I must also recommend the book *Bergsonism* (1988) for the voracious reader, as well.

Gebser's corroborative aperspectival thinkers, such as Teilhard's writings on evolution and planetization (*The Phenomenon of Man*, 1955), a mysticism of matter (*The Hymn of the Universe*, 1961), and Sri Aurobindo Ghose (*The Life Divine*, 1939 and *The Integral Yoga* letters, 1993) are necessary texts for the serious reader.

I would be remiss to abstain from suggesting that the reader encounter the poems of Rainer Maria Rilke, and so *Sonnets to Orpheus* (2015), translated by Gebserian scholar Daniel Joseph Polikoff, as well as Polikoff's biography, *In the Image of Orpheus: Rilke—A Soul History* (2011) are recommended.

As a complement to Gebser's exploration of perspectivalism, John Berger's classic *Ways of Seeing* (1990) is recommended. Finally, Marshall McLuhan—and media studies as a field—is an excellent companion to reading into Gebser's structures. *The Gutenberg Galaxy: The Making of Typographic Man* (1962) and *Understanding Media: The Extensions of Man* (1964) are classics that should be read in *any* study of cultural evolution.[10]

---

10 It might be said that media studies, as developed by McLuhan, *is* an aperspectival field: it is the move from looking at items in the environment to a study of the environmental surround itself.

Integral Florilegium

This section deserves to be expanded into its own text, as a thorough study of the manifestations of integral consciousness in our time is beyond the scope of this introductory volume. Nevertheless, a few integral "flowerings" must be pointed out.

Eugene Thacker's philosophical book series, starting with *In the Dust of This Planet: Horror of Philosophy* (2011) is an interesting development in exploring the arational and conceptualizing the more than human world. Similarly, Graham Harman's *Object-Oriented Ontology: A New Theory of Everything* (2018), and Timothy Morton's *Hyperobjects: Philosophy and Ecology After the End of the World* (2013) move mental conceptualizations of the objective world into stranger territories and should be read as a trend towards aperspectival thinking. Morton's recent *Being Ecological* (2018) reads as a text that fundamentally breaks perspectival anthropocentrism.

Moving from scholarship to art, if there is a text that we believe embodies integral consciousness, it would be the Taoist anarchism inspired science fiction of Ursula K Le Guin: *The Dispossessed: An Ambiguous Utopia* (1974) which examines freedom in an anarchic society, and *The Lathe of Heaven* (1971), which explores dreaming, (mental) control, and reality. Le Guin's Taoist

anarchism mirrors Gebser's own emphasis on replac-
ing the mental structure's "goal-oriented, purposive
thought" with an integral "unintentionality."[11] Concerning an integral temporics, Le Guin's opening essay
to *Always Coming Home* (1985), "Towards an Arche-
ology of the Future," asks: "Which is farther from us,
farther out of reach, more silent—the dead, or the un-
born?"[12] Lastly, Le Guin's translation of *Lao Tzu: Tao Te
Ching: A Book About the Way and the Power of the Way*
(1998) is recommended as a contemplative companion
for the integral reader.

If Timothy Morton's hyperobjects are a move toward the aperspectival in philosophy and ecology, then
Jeff VanderMeer's *Annihilation* (2014) and the Southern Reach trilogy deserves equal attention as a literary
equivalent. The novel describes investigations into a
strange zone, Area X, which could easily be described as
a hyperobject. Rather than human beings figuring out
what Area X ultimately is, Area X, in some sense, sub-
sumes *us*. As one reviewer writes, "Area X represents
not ecological collapse but rather *human* collapse—or,

---

11 Feuerstein, *Structures of Consciousness*, 170.

12 Ursula K. Le Guin, *Always Coming Home* (Berkeley: University of
    California Press, 1985), 4.

better said, human transmutation."[13] The text is something of a catalytic reading itself, producing moments
of phenomenological receptivity in the reader to encounter the natural world not as mythical images nor
as a magical nexus but as strange, unknowable encounters with singularities, and diaphanous beings.

Many more creative works could be noted, but it is
sufficient to state that in each of them a planetized tomorrow is being expressed in the cultural imagination
of the present. Gebser's own work, *Ever-Present Origin*
is just such an anticipatory—prefigurative—text.[14]
Fiction, or non-fiction does not matter in this regard;
integrality expresses freedom of the "open expanse of
the open world."[15] We can encounter it in many ways.

---

13 David Tompkins, "Weird Ecology: On the Southern Reach Tril-
    ogy," *Los Angeles Review of Books*: https://lareviewofbooks.org/
    article/weird-ecology-southern-reach-trilogy/ [last accessed 1
    Dec 2018].

14 David Runciman, "The Democracy Project: a History, a Crisis, a
    Movement by David Graeber—Review," *The Guardian*: https://
    www.theguardian.com/books/2013/mar/28/democracy-proj-
    ect-david-graeber-review [last accessed 1 Dec 2018]. Referring to
    Graeber's "prefigurative politics," Runciman writes, "protests are
    not meant to extract concessions from the existing system, but to
    give people an idea of what the world would be like if there was
    no system and individuals were free to make their own choices."
    I borrow "prefigurative" to align Gebser's temporics of integral
    freedom with the project of democratic freedom (which is not
    merely political anarchism or any "ism" but a spiritual project).

15 Feuerstein, *Structures of Consciousness*, 170.

When we respond to this originary freedom (which we already *have*, already *are*) with the creative urgency of mutational leaps—momentary irruptions of a planetary future—we learn the necessary lessons to more truly substantiate the integral world.

Bibliography

Balter, Michael. *The Goddess and the Bull: Catalhoyuk: An Archaeological Journey to the Dawn of Civilization*. New York: Free Press, 2006.

Banerji, Debashish. *Seven Quartets of Becoming: A Transformative Yoga Psychology Based on the Diaries of Sri Aurobindo*. New Delhi: D. K. Printworld, 2012.

Barfield, Owen. *Saving the Appearances*. Hanover: University Press of New England, 1988.

Baruss, Imants. *Alterations of Consciousness: An Empirical Analysis for Social Scientists*. Washington DC: American Psychological Association, 2004.

Bateson, Nora. *Small Arcs of Larger Circles: Framing Through Other Patterns*. Axminster: Triarchy Press, 2016.

Benjamin, Walter. *Illuminations*. New York: Shocken Books, 2007.

Bridle, James. *New Dark Age: Technology and the End of the Future*. Brooklyn: Verso, 2018.

Canavan, Gerry. "'There's Nothing New / Under The Sun, / But There Are New Suns': Recovering Octavia E. Butler's Lost Parables," *Los Angeles Review of Books*: https://lareviewofbooks. org/article/theres-nothing-new-sun-new-suns-recovering- octavia-e-butlers-lost-parables/

Cook, Jill. "The Lion Man: An Ice Age Masterpiece": https://blog. britishmuseum.org/the-lion-man-an-ice-age-masterpiece/

Deleuze, Gilles, and Félix Guattari. *Anti-Oedipus: Capitalism and Schizophrenia*. Minneapolis: University of Minnesota Press, 1983.

———. *What is Philosophy?* New York: Columbia UP, 1994.

———. *A Thousand Plateaus: Capitalism and Schizophrenia*. New York: Continuum, 2003.

———, and Claire Parnet, *Dialogues*. New York: Columbia UP, 2002.

Ebert, John David. *The New Media Invasion: Digital Technologies and the World They Unmake*. Jefferson: McFarrland, 2011.

———. *The Age of Catastrophe: Disaster and Humanity in Modern Times*. Jefferson: McFarland, 2012.

Feuerstein, Georg. *Structures of Consciousness*. Lower Lake: Integral Publishing, 1987.

Fisher, Mark. *Ghosts of My Life*. Alesford: Zero Books, 2014.

Ford, Phil, J.F. Martel, and Michael Garfield. "Living in a Glass Age, with Michael Garfield." *Weird Studies*. https://www.weird-studies.com/26

Gebser, Jean. *The Ever-Present Origin*, trans. Noel Barstad with Algis Mickunas. Athens, OH: University of Ohio Press, 1997.

———. Preface to *Verfall und Teilhabe*. In Feuerstein, *Structures of Consciousness*, 1987.

———, and Scott Preston. "Jean Gebser and Integral Consciousness: The Inaugural Post." http://blog.gebser.net/2012/01/jean-gebser-integral-consciousness.html

Graeber, David. "Occupy Wall Street's Anarchist Roots." *Al Jazeera*. https://www.aljazeera.com/indepth/opinion/2011/11/201111287283590408.html

Gray, John. "Steven Pinker is wrong about violence and war." *The Guardian*. https://www.theguardian.com/books/2015/mar/13/john-gray-steven-pinker-wrong-violence-war-declining

Grossman, Pam. *Waking the Witch: Reflections on Women, Magic and Power*. New York: Gallery Books, 2019.

Grusin, Richard. *The Non-Human Turn*. Minneapolis: University of Minnesota Press, 2015.

Hardt, Michael, and Antonio Negri. *Multitude: War and Democracy in the Age of Empire*. New York: Penguin, 2004.

Jaynes, Julian. *The Origins of Consciousness in the Breakdown of the Bicameral Mind*. New York: Houghton Mifflin Harcourt, 1990.

Kelly, Kevin. *Out of Control: The New Biology of Machines, Social Systems and the Economic World*. New York: Basic Books, 1994.

———. *What Technology Wants*. New York: Penguin Books, 2010.

Kofman, Ava. "Bruno Latour, the Post-Truth Philosopher, Mounts a Defense of Science." *New York Times*: https://www.nytimes.com/2018/10/25/magazine/bruno-latour-post-truth-philosopher-science.html

Le Guin, Ursula K. *Always Coming Home*. Berkeley: University of California Press, 1985.

———. *Late in the Day: Poems 2010–2014*. Oakland: PM Press, 2016. Kindle edition.

Luna, Luis Eduardo, and Pablo Amaringo. *Ayahuasca Visions: The Religious Iconography of a Peruvian Shaman*. Berkeley: North Atlantic Books, 1999.

Martel, J.F. *Reclaiming Art in the Age of Artifice: A Treatise, Critique and Call to Action*. Berkeley: Evolver Editions, 2015.

McKenna, Terrence. *The Archaic Revival*. San Francisco: Harper Collins, 1991.

McLuhan, Marshall. *Understanding Media: The Extensions of Man*. Cambridge, MA: MIT Press, 1994.

Morton, Timothy. *Hyperobjects: Philosophy and Ecology after the End of the World*. Minneapolis: University of Minnesota Press, 2013.

———. *Dark Ecology: For a Logic of Future Coexistence*. New York: Columbia UP, 2016.

———. *Being Ecological*. Cambridge, MA: MIT Press, 2018.

Papova, Maria. "Networked Knowledge and Combinatorial Creativity," *Brain Pickings*: www.brainpickings.org/2011/08/01/networked-knowledge-combinatorial-creativity/

Pico della Mirandola, Giovanni. *Oration on the Dignity of Man*, ed. and trans. Francesco Borghesi, Michael Papio, and Massimo Riva. Cambridge: Cambridge UP, 2012.

Runciman, David. "The Democracy Project: a History, a Crisis, a Movement by David Graeber—Review." *The Guardian*. https://www.theguardian.com/books/2013/mar/28/democracy-project-david-graeber-review

Rushkoff, Douglas. *Throwing Rocks at the Google Bus*. New York: Portfolio/Penguin, 2017.

Sample, Ian. "Neanderthals Built Mysterious Cave Structures 175,000 Years Ago." *The Guardian*. https://www.theguardian.com/science/2016/may/25/neanderthals-built-mysterious-cave-structures-175000-years-ago

Shlain. Leonard. *The Alphabet Versus the Goddess*. New York: Penguin/Compass, 1998.

Sloterdijk, Peter. *You Must Change Your Life*. Malden: Polity Press, 2013.

Tarnas, Richard. *The Passion of the Western Mind*. New York: Random House, 1991.

———. *Cosmos and Psyche*. New York: Penguin, 2006.

Tart, Charles. *The End of Materialism: How Evidence of the Paranormal is Bringing Science and Spirit Together*. Oakland: New Harbinger, 2009.

Teilhard de Chardin, Pierre. *Hymn of the Universe*. New York: Perennial, 1972.

Thacker, Eugene. *In The Dust of This Planet*. Alesford: Zero Books, 2011.

Thompson, William Irwin. *Passages About Earth: An Exploration of the New Planetary Culture*. New York: Harper & Row, 1974.

———. *Pacific Shift*. San Francisco: Sierra Club, 1985.

———. *The Time Falling Bodies Take to Light: Mythology, Sexuality and the Origins of Culture*. New York: Saint Martin's Press, 1996.

———. *Coming Into Being: Artifacts and Texts in the Evolution of Consciousness*. New York: St. Martin's Griffin, 1996.

———. *Self and Society: Studies in the Evolution of Culture*. Exeter: Imprint Academic, 2009.

Tolkien, J.R.R. "Mythopoeia," in *Tree and Leaf, including the Poem Mythopeia*. Boston: Houghton Mufflin, 1988.

Tompkins, David. "Weird Ecology: On the Southern Reach Trilogy." *Los Angeles Review of Books*. https://lareviewofbooks.org/article/weird-ecology-southern-reach-trilogy/

Toulmin, Stephen. "The Inwardness of Mental Life." *Critical Inquiry* 6.1 (1979): 1–16.

Virilio, Paul. *Speed and Politics*. Los Angeles: Semiotext(e), 2007.

Wahlquist, Calla. "A Life in Quotes: Ursula K Le Guin." *The Guardian*. https://www.theguardian.com/books/2018/jan/24/a-life-in-quotes-ursula-k-le-guin

Webb, Hillary S. *Yanantin and Masintin in the Andean World: Complementary Dualism in Modern Peru*. Albuquerque: University of New Mexico Press, 2009.

Wilber, Ken. *The Collected Works of Ken Wilber, Volume 2*. Boston: Shambhala, 1999.

Zakroff, Laura Tempest, ed., *The New Aradia: A Witch's Handbook to Magical Resistance*. Seattle: Revelore Press, 2018.

About Nura Learning

NURA LEARNING SPRUNG UP in 2017 as a
virtual learning space to unite the constella-
tions of imaginal studies, consciousness studies, and integral philosophy. It was inspired by both the
contemporary and historical brick-and-mortar alternative institutions such as the California Institute of
Integral Studies, Goddard College (my alma mater),
Auroville, and the Lindisfarne Association, building
in whatever humble way towards a new planetary culture. Integral to the generation of new culture is new
education and the production of new forms of art,
aesthetics, and knowledge-making. *Nuralogicals* were
created to extend the virtual classroom back into embodied space and place—passed from hand to hand, or
bookshelf-to-bookshelf, in the spirit of the rhizomatic
zine!—and offer another form of incarnation for some
of the brilliant insights made by our learning community. For this reason, I am delighted to partner with
Revelore Press to produce these texts, which allows
our teachers to also becomes authors, just as literature

allows culture to write itself into reality. *Nuralogicals* are produced by our faculty and serve as companion readers before, during, and after their digital counterparts.

This book was written *before* my class in the winter of 2019, and so it is, as Gebser would say, *latent*. The Nura Learning course, "Seeing Through the World: Reading Jean Gebser and Ever-Present Origin," however, will be offered annually each winter—appropriately timed when Gebser himself was poetically inspired in the winter of 1944, and later, when he completed *EPO* in the winter of 1949—and so if you are holding this book in your hand sometime between course offerings, consider joining us for the next course. Psychoactive and spiritually potent texts—catalytic readings—are better done in the context of *hyper*text. In other words, they are better read together.

In the fall of 2018, Dr. Becca S. Tarnas, of the California Institute of Integral Studies, hosted the highly engaged and successful Nura Learning class, "Journey to the Imaginal Realm: Reading J.R.R. Tolkien's *The Lord of the Rings*." Dr. Tarnas draws deeply from both Tolkien's theological insights on the concept of sub-creation and C.G. Jung's gnostic and imaginal perspectives on archetypal reality to perform an exegesis on one of the most widely read books of the twentieth century. Her book, *Journey to the Imaginal Realm: Reading J.R.R. Tolkien's*

The Lord of the Rings (2019) is an adaptation of the class lectures and, like this book, you can take it with you on your literary sojourn into the primary text.

I am enthusiastic that the first two *Nuralogicals* seem to be drawing upon certain commonalities, and that Nura Learning and Revelore, in corroboration, are drawn to teaching and publishing on the significance of imaginal insight. Whether it is Tolkien's Eru Ilúvatar, or Gebser's creative and spiritual *Urpsrung*, a movement of consciousness towards self-realization and creative concretization is taking place; and so, perhaps, you should revisit Tolkien's twentieth-century classic in this new light.

Jeremy Johnson
St. Petersburg, FL
5 January 2019

CPSIA information can be obtained
at www.ICGtesting.com
Printed in the USA
LVHW090628030320
648720LV00002B/188